ANDREW J. BANDSTRA

S0-AZR-763

in the company of
ANGELS

WHAT THE BIBLE TEACHES
WHAT YOU NEED TO KNOW

Vine Books
Servant Publications
Ann Arbor, Michigan

Cover: *Death and Assumption of Virgin* —Fra Angelico (1387-1455)

Abbreviations used:
NIV (New International Version)
NRSV (New Revised Standard Version)
RSV (Revised Standard Version)

Unless otherwise noted, the Scripture quotations in this book are from the HOLY BIBLE, NEW INTERNATIONAL VERSION, copyright 1973, 1978, 1984, International Bible Society. Used by permission of Zondervan Bible Publishers.

Vine Books is an imprint of Servant Publications especially designed to serve Evangelical Christians.

Copyright © 1995 by CRC Publications, 2850 Kalamazoo SE, Grand Rapids, Michigan 49560. Copublished with Servant Publications, P.O. Box 8617 Ann Arbor, Michigan 48107.

Library of Congress Cataloging-in-Publication Data
Bandstra, Andrew, 1926-
     In the company of angels: what the Bible teaches: what you need to know /
  Andrew Bandstra.
       p. cm.
     Includes bibliographical references.
     ISBN 0-89283-922-8
     1. Angels—Biblical teaching. I. Title.
    [BS680.A48B36   1995]
    235'.3—dc20   95-2439
                                                CIP

10 9 8 7 6 5 4 3 2

With joy, dedicated to
Nancy Stob, Ruth Bandstra, Sue Hamstra,
Mary Ippel, and Barbara Newman

CONTENTS

PREFACE

The writing of a book, even a small one, involves a kind of paradox. Writing is at the same time both a very individualistic process and an intensely communal one: individualistic because it involves hours alone with the word processor; communal because the writer is indebted to so many persons for what is written. A preface is a handy instrument to acknowledge and thank the many people of the community for their help.

Thanks to CRC Publications and in particular Harvey Smit for suggesting that I write such a book. Also thanks to Servant Publications and in particular Ann Spangler for expressing interest in the project and for agreeing to copublish it. Without their interest and prodding the book would probably not have been written.

I owe much to my colleagues at Calvin Theological Seminary for their collegial spirit and helpfulness over many years of teaching together. Special mention should be made of John Wesley Cooper, who discussed with me the philosophical and theological background of some writers on the subject of angels, and to J. Marion Snapper, who suggested some bibliography in the area of angels and the biblical narrative.

Speaking of bibliography, I have not included in it the *Summa Theologica* of St. Thomas Aquinas, even though, like most who write on the subject of angels in the Christian tradition, I am indebted to his writing. I judged that his work might be too "philosophical" for many readers of this book who are interested in a more narrowly "biblical" study.

At the other end of the spectrum, I have included few titles of those writing about angels from the "new age" perspective. Such books go well beyond the biblical perspective that is being attempted in this book. But I do thank those authors for aiding and abetting a renewed interest in angelology.

Included in the bibliography is only one commentary on a biblical book—John Calvin on Hebrews—from which I quoted directly. But I am much indebted to many scholars and their comments on relevant biblical texts. To include all of them in the bibliography would make it much too long. So I'll take this opportunity to say thanks to all of you for your help and insights.

My thanks also to the many church groups to whom, over the course of the years, I presented much of this material and from whom I have gained many helpful insights. The last of these helpful encounters was a six-week lecture series at the church in Rehoboth, New Mexico.

A special word of thanks to family members: To our sons-in-law, who showed interest in the subject and suggested material relevant for this study. To my wife, Mae, who devoted many hours to helping with the proofreading. And to our five daughters, to whom I have dedicated this book and who over the years have given and continue to give us much joy. That joy comes from many things, not the least of which is the fact that each of them is committed to doing what the hymn writer calls "angels' work below."

The writer of Psalm 148 calls upon all creatures in heaven and on earth to give praise to the Lord: "all his angels . . . all his heavenly hosts" and "from the earth . . . young men and maidens, old men and children." That includes the writer of this book on the biblical teaching about angels. *Gloria in excelsis Deo!*

The Annunciation

—Zeleke Iwunetu

CHAPTER 1

WHY STUDY ABOUT ANGELS?

It was a cold, wintry Michigan night. Snow had been falling since early afternoon, and road conditions were poor. But Evan and his friend decided to go to the mall anyway. Christmas was only a week away, and they might not get another chance to shop for gifts for their wives.

As the two men drove carefully along snow-covered roads, they came across a stalled car. It was obvious that the young driver needed help, so Evan and his friend struggled to push the car off the road.

Meanwhile, another car was approaching on the icy roadway. The driver didn't see the two men and the stalled car until it was too late to stop. But as the car swerved on the ice toward the two men, someone (Evan knows that it was an angel) led Evan to turn around. That warning gave the two men just the time they needed to jump into the snowbank before the moving car slammed into the rear of the disabled car. Evan and his friend were unharmed.

Today Evan is serving in the ministry of the gospel. Many things went into preparing Evan for gospel ministry, but he knows that one of them was the mighty intervention of an angel on that snowy winter night in Michigan.

Evan's story is an "angel story." Many Christians have such stories to tell, and many have shared those stories with me over the years. People who have had encounters with angels are generally eager to talk about them because such encounters always have a profound impact on a person's life.

A variety of recent books about angels describe encounters like Evan's. Many of them are good books, filled with stories that offer encouragement and strength to other Christians. You will find some of them listed in the bibliography at the end of this book.

But most of these books do not address the *biblical* teaching about angels, and that's unfortunate. Christian experience is most authentic and helpful to others when it coincides with the biblical message. Our Christian experience is to be normed by the Bible, the Word of God.

This book is a small attempt to lay out the teachings of the Bible concerning angels. I hope it will be helpful—both to those who have angel stories to tell and to those who do not.

Angels in the Bible

Seminary professors enjoy telling the story about a professor who held a brief session of his theology class one week: "Today, the subject for discussion is 'angels,'" he told the group. "I don't know anything about angels. Class dismissed."

Although this story is no doubt apocryphal, it illustrates an important point: Many people feel that they really know next to nothing about angels.

That ignorance is understandable from one point of view: many good Christians do not have angel stories to tell. But from another point of view it is very surprising: the Bible has a lot to say about angels. Although not every book of the Bible includes references to angels, angels do make regular appearances in Scripture. Some of the following angel facts may surprise people who think they are "ignorant" about angels:

- The book of Revelation makes at least sixty-seven references to an angel or to angels.

- All of the New Testament authors refer to angels.

- Though the word *angel* does not appear in every single one of Paul's books, he uses the term at least fourteen times.

But although the Bible includes frequent mention of angels, it stops short of offering a theological explanation for these heavenly beings. Hebrews 1 and 2 come the closest to providing a kind of "theology" of angels, but even there the writer's primary purpose is to show that angels, as great as they are, are subordinate to Jesus Christ, the God/Man.

The Bible does help us understand something about who or what angels are and what they do under God's sovereign control. That biblical understanding is the focus of this book.

The Company We Keep

Why study about angels? Well, for one thing it's a lot safer to study about angels than about demons! The Bible suggests that a person is known by the company she or he keeps. And it is a lot wiser to be known as a person who keeps company with angels than one who keeps company with demons. The church father Thomas Aquinas was known as *doctor angelicus*, or "angelic doctor," in part, at least, because he wrote so much about angels. That's a lot better than being known as *doctor daemonicus*, or "demonic doctor."

Very seriously, sometimes people who spend a lot of time studying about the devil or demons get caught up in their power and end up in a satanic cult—much to the detriment of their spiritual well-being. Karl Barth, the same theologian who said that when we speak about angels, we should do so only "softly and incidentally," claims that we should never look at the devil or demons too long or too intently. He suggests that such familiarity has never done anyone any good, and could do a person (even a person like Martin Luther, who is said to have thrown an inkwell at the devil!) considerable harm. In that sense it is certainly safer to study about angels.

But there is a second important reason why we are pursuing this study about angels, and it has to do with our own ignorance: in general, the devil gets more than his due. Christians seem to know more about the devil and demons than they do about angels. Author Hope MacDonald states that while she was staying in Scotland one summer, she and her husband visited one of the larger bookstores. They noticed shelf after shelf of books about the devil and the occult, but not one book in the entire store about angels.

Of course, it is necessary to know what the Bible has to say about our archenemy, Satan. We need to be aware that Jesus, the "strong man," came to bind the devil in order to rob the devil of his possessions (Matt.12:29). It is crucial to understand that Jesus came to destroy the works of the devil (1 John 3:8). Our warfare against the principalities and the world ruler of wickedness in high places is possible because we can take our stand in Jesus, who has already won the initial and decisive victory over the devil (Eph. 6:10-13). Too often we might think that victory over the demonic forces is up to us—but if we try to do battle with demons in our own strength, we will fail. We can only be victorious by trusting in the victory that Jesus himself won over the devil and his hosts.

Thus, it is important to know what the Bible says about the devil and the occult. But, as Billy Graham has reminded us, the angels have a much more important place in the Bible than the devil and his demons do. If that is true, and I believe that it is, then we Christians ought to study what the Bible has to say about the legions of angels at God's command.

Another theologian, John Calvin, reminds us that when we affirm the existence of angels and study diligently what the Bible has to say about them, we must be careful not to fall into superstition. He meant especially that we ought not to transfer to them the power, honor, and glory that belong to God and Christ alone.

The author of Hebrews says that angels are not on the same level as God or as Jesus, the God/Man (Heb. 1 and 2). God not only created the world (including the angels) but also, through his Son Jesus, accomplished our redemption. Even as the God/Man, crucified and glorified at God's right hand, Jesus is over the angels (Heb. 2:5-9). Angels are, therefore, (only) "ministering spirits sent to serve those who will inherit salvation" (Heb.1:14). God and Jesus are in the center of things; angels belong only to the periphery. So we speak about them, as Barth suggested, "softly and incidentally."

Calvin gives us some further good advice to guide us in our study about angels. He notes that we should avoid what he calls empty speculation concerning the nature, orders, and number of angels. Often, he warns us, people are more interested in such speculation than in what the Bible clearly and actually says. Thus, in the history of the church, theologians allegedly paid a lot of attention to the question of how many angels could dance on the head of a pin. Such speculation is superfluous to what the Scriptures teach us about the Lord's angels.

Incidentally, two recent scholars, Mortimer Adler and Geddes MacGregor, have cast doubt on whether discussion about how many angels can dance on the head of a pin ever took place. To date, at least, there seems to be no text in medieval literature that suggests such discussion. Adler himself thinks that modern scoffers invented this story about medieval theologians in order to give a negative image to the study of angels.

Unfortunately, it appears that the scoffers have largely succeeded in poisoning the minds of many against the serious consideration of angels. All the more reason to keep rather strictly to what the Bible says and away from empty speculation.

What You Will Find in This Study

The Nature of Angels

In spite of warnings from both Calvin and Barth that the Bible doesn't really tell us about the "nature" of angels, we are devoting two brief chapters to that subject. Chapter 2 includes what I think the Scriptures suggest about the "nature" of angels, and chapter 3 presents a discussion of the names and titles that the Bible uses for these beings.

I believe we may speak about the "nature" of angels insofar as the Bible clearly does so. You will have to be the judge as to whether we succeed. Furthermore, it seems to me that both Barth and Calvin affirm some things about the "being" of angels even though they hesitate to speak of the "nature" of angels. For example, Barth says that the Bible teaches that the angels are *created* beings. They are not gods, but belong with humanity on this side of the great divide between the Creator and creation. It is that sort of thing that I mean when I refer to the "nature" of angels—the intrinsic characteristics or qualities of angels described in the Bible.

Of course, "nature" can be used in a more detailed and comprehensive sense to refer to the order, disposition, and essence that compose something. I suspect it is "nature" used in that way that Barth and Calvin are warning against. Scripture does not give us that kind of detailed analysis of the "nature" of angels.

The Function of Angels

The second part of the book is devoted to a study of the "function" of angels. What "job description" does the Bible lay out for them? Here also it will be important to try to think the thoughts of the Bible and not to go beyond what is written.

Of course, there will be times when scholars disagree about what the Bible says. For example, in Galatians 4:3 (cf. also v. 9) and Colossians 2:8 and 20, Paul uses a phrase that originally meant in certain circles, "the elements of the world." But what did *Paul* mean by it? The RSV translates the phrase as "the elemental spirits of the universe." If that is the meaning, then the references should be considered under the general category of "angels" (or, as some think, "demons"). But if (as I tried to prove already in my doctoral dissertation, *The Law and the Elements of the World*) the phrase means something like "the basic principles of the world" (see also the NIV translation), then the reference is most probably not to angels and therefore should not be considered in this study.

In discussing the "function" of angels, it will be important to remember that, as holy angels who are ministers of God, the angels never do anything "on their own." They only do what God wants and assigns them to do. Some people, in thinking about the function of angels, employ a kind of "business model." They think of God as the chief executive officer who has granted significant authority to the angels as "department heads." They imagine that angels have a kind of self-rule or autonomy of their own "to get the work done." But this model doesn't apply. Angels do not work autonomously. As God's ambassadors or envoys, they speak and do everything that God wants them to. Although angels are not "heavenly robots," they never function "on their own."

The Belief in Angels

How should angels function, if at all, in our faith life? What are some of the dangers we should avoid in considering this belief in angels? Those are some of the questions we will look at in the third part of this study. Many good Christians who acknowledge that angels exist are nevertheless not truly aware of them and do not orient their lives in regard to them. What *should* our posture be? To put the question in a slightly different way: what profit or benefit do or should Christian believers derive from believing in angels?

Here we are attempting to be true to John Calvin, who insisted that with regard to angels [and all other things for that matter], Christian theologians should teach only those things that are "true and sure," "profitable," or "beneficial." He rightly insists that if the doctrine of angels is not profitable or beneficial to our faith, then there is no good reason to devote time and attention to studying these beings.

Determining things that are "true, sure, and beneficial" about angels is a big order. Yet with that goal in mind, let us commence our study of what the Bible has to say about angels.

Angel

—Lucas Van Leyden (1494-1533)

CHAPTER 2

WHAT ANGELS ARE LIKE

We may never consider the "nature" of angels in the abstract, only in the context of the work they do. Angels are ambassadors in God's kingdom who take part in God's revelation throughout history. For example, immediately after the story of Jesus' baptism, Mark's gospel records the following: "At once the Spirit sent him [Jesus] out into the desert, and he was in the desert forty days, being tempted by Satan. He was with the wild animals, and angels attended him" (Mark 1:12-13). Mark does not explain what the angels did in attending or ministering to Jesus—they are simply a part of the gospel story about Jesus' victory over Satan.

How closely the ministry of angels is tied into the coming of the kingdom of God is evident from the verses that immediately follow in Mark's gospel: "After John was put in prison, Jesus went into Galilee, proclaiming the good news of God. 'The time has come,' he said. 'The Kingdom of God is near. Repent and believe the good news.'"

It's important to keep this image of angels as kingdom ambassadors in mind as we explore what the Bible reveals about these beings.

Spiritual Beings

In a passage comparing and contrasting angels with the eternal Son of God, the author of Hebrews concludes with a rhetorical question: "Are not all angels ministering spirits sent to serve those who will inherit salvation?" (Heb. 1:14). It's a question that expects an affirmative response: "Yes, all angels are such ministering spirits."

There you have it: angels are "spirits" who "minister."

Please bear with me while I say something a little bit complicated about this text. Some Bible interpreters argue that we shouldn't make so much of the term "spirits" in this verse. The accent seems to be on the fact that angels are *ministering* spirits, these interpreters contend, because the text goes on to say that angels are sent to serve or minister to believers.

Hebrews 1:14 *does* stress ministry, but that doesn't mean that the reference to angels as spirits is unimportant. I think the writer wanted his readers to know that angels are "spirits" as well as "ministers." You see, verse 14 is actually a conclusion based on Psalm 104:4, which is quoted in Hebrews 1:7. There the author of Hebrews understands the psalmist to say (based on the Greek or Septuagint text of the Old Testament): "He makes his angels winds [literally: he makes his angels *spirits*], his servants [or: ministers] flames of fire." By calling angels "ministering spirits," therefore, the author of Hebrews is using and giving equal importance to the two main ideas that he found in the Greek text of Psalm 104:4.

So much for the complicated part. Right now we are interested in the fact that angels are spirits; we will come back to their "ministry" in the second part of this book.

I am comforted to note that John Calvin, who warned against all idle speculation about the "nature" of angels, nonetheless affirms, on the basis of this text, that angels are spirits who really exist. That is, angels are not merely "ideas" or "impulses," but spirits of real substance. Otherwise, says Calvin, the arguments of the author of Hebrews do not make sense.

Since angels are spirits, it's probable that they lack bodily form and are usually not visible to the physical eye. Note that Paul, in Colossians 1:16, seems to equate "things in heaven" with the things "invisible," which clearly refers to the principalities and powers.

Nevertheless, in the Bible angels often assume bodily shape to witness to God's gospel story. Consider these examples:

- Abraham "saw" three men standing near his tent under the great trees of Mamre (Gen.18:1-2). Only later do we find out that they were angels from the Lord God who had a hand in the destruction of Sodom and Gomorrah (Gen.19:1).

- According to Mark's gospel, the woman entering the tomb "saw" a young man dressed in a white robe sitting on the right side (Mark 16:5).

- According to Matthew's gospel, it was an angel of the Lord who rolled away the stone, sat on it, and spoke to the women (Matt. 28:2-7).

But these seem to be only temporary appearances on special occasions.

Created Beings

The Bible treats angels as part of the created order. In other words, they stand with us as created beings, in contrast to God, who is the Creator. To be sure, angels are not mentioned in the accounts of creation given in Genesis 1-3. So we have no account of *when* they were created. Theologians, both Jewish and Christian, have speculated about associating the creation of angels with one or another of the "days" of creation. Augustine thought it was the first day—associating angels with "light." But Calvin pleaded for caution and sobriety in such matters, insisting that the *time* of their creation is really not important.

The Bible treats angels as part of the "heavenly" yet created world. For example, in Psalm 148 the poet speaks in a powerful way of angels, heavenly hosts, sun, moon, stars, and so on—calling upon all of them to praise God. And he says of them (v. 5): "for [God] commanded and they were created." And in good New Testament fashion, Paul affirms in a hymn-like section that all things, visible and invisible, things in heaven and things on earth were created "in," "by" and "for" the Son, who is the image of the invisible God and the firstborn over all creation (Col.1:15-17). Although Paul does not mention the word "angels" in that hymn, he does specifically refer to "thrones, rulers, powers, and authorities." These terms were used in the Jewish literature of that time to designate angelic beings. We will come back to those designations in chapter 10. Here it is important to see that all things in heaven and on earth, including angelic beings, belong to the created order.

To use only one more text, in Romans 8:38-39 Paul states that he is persuaded that nothing will be able to separate us from the love of God in Christ Jesus our Lord. He mentions such things as death and life, present and future, height and depth, and also includes angels, principalities, and powers. He then adds: "nor anything else in all creation." Clearly Paul sees all of the forces mentioned there, including angels, as part of the created order.

It's important to keep in mind that angels are *created* beings. John Calvin worried that Christians might too quickly become superstitious and attribute to angels the glory that should be given to God alone. If people begin to think that angels are really the dispensers of blessings, Calvin maintained, they might quickly fall down and worship them.

In the book of Revelation, John also seems concerned about people worshiping angels (angels do, after all, play a great role in that book). John says that after the angel gave him his commission to write, he [John] fell at his feet to worship him (Rev. 19:10). But the angel reprimanded him: "Do not do it! I am a fellow servant with you and with your brothers who hold to the testimony of Jesus. Worship God!" Almost exactly the same experience is recounted in Revelation 22:8-9. We are not to worship angels— God alone is worthy of our worship.

Limited Beings

The first two characteristics—that angels are *created spirits*—are the most important and basic of the description the Bible gives us. The other three characteristics that we will look at in this chapter are more peripheral and can be deduced from these first two.

Clearly, the truth that angels are "limited" beings really is part and parcel of their nature as created beings. Yet there has been some controversy and dispute over the character of these limitations.

We confess that God is "all-knowing, all-powerful and every-where present." By way of contrast, angels are created beings and are therefore not all-knowing or all-powerful or everywhere present. But the Bible doesn't directly speak about these limitations, so we had best be careful here lest Barth and Calvin clobber us for idle speculation about the "nature" of angels.

In considering the evidence, we may not always get a consistent picture of angels in the Bible. For example, on the one hand, Jacob, while at Luz (later called Bethel), had a dream of a stairway or ladder stretching from earth to heaven. According to Genesis 28:12 the angels of God were ascending and descending on the ladder. On the other hand, some angels are said to have wings (cherubim and seraphim), and these angels are said to "fly" (Dan. 9:21; Rev. 14:6). If angels fly, it is not easy to understand why they would need a ladder, is it? Yet, in one important way these images (the ladder, wings, flying) agree: they all make clear that angels are limited with respect to space; they are not everywhere present.

Nor are angels all-powerful. As creatures, they operate by divine authority: they do what God commands them to do. The psalmist exhorts: "Praise the LORD, you his angels, you mighty ones who do his bidding, who obey his word" (Ps. 103:20). Daniel 10-12 gives the somewhat perplexing account about "the one who looked like a man" and who is yet described more like an angel (Dan. 10:4-6). This "man" states that he had been sent in response to Daniel's prayer for understanding but on the way was detained for twenty-one days by the "prince of Persia." Fortunately for both Daniel and the "one who looked like a man," Michael, one of the chief princes, helped the "man" against the resistance of the "prince of Persia" (Dan. 10:12-14).

Even though angels are heavenly creatures, they are also limited in their knowledge. Jesus says about the coming of the Son of Man: "No one knows about that day or hour, not even the angels in heaven, nor the Son, but only the Father" (Mark 13:32). The fact that the Scriptures say that even "the Son" does not know the time of the coming of the Son of Man presents something of a theological problem. Christians most often understand this verse to refer to Jesus in his human nature as distinct from his divine nature. But for our purposes we note that "even the angels in heaven" do not know the day or hour of Christ's coming.

Peter says something to the same effect (1 Pet. 1:10-12). He magnifies the insight given to the prophets about the salvation that ultimately came through Jesus Christ and that was preached in the gospel. This discernment given to the prophets was so great that it surpassed the knowledge of angels, as Peter implies when he concludes: "even angels long to look into these things."

Holy Beings

Three times the New Testament refers to "holy angels" (Matt. 25:31; Luke 9:26; and Rev.14:10). It could be that these verses refer to a special class of angels. At least one Jewish book of the intertestamentary times (the book of Jubilees) refers to three groups of angels: the angels of the Presence, the angels of Holiness, and the angels in charge of everyday affairs. Thus it's possible that in the New Testament "holy angels" might also refer to a special class of angels, such as the "angels of Holiness."

But it is more likely that Jesus (in Matthew and Luke) is simply describing one characteristic of all angels: they are beings who have been set aside to serve God. Holiness, as you may recall, does not refer so much to a moral quality as it does to separation for the service of God. Angels are creatures, as Psalm 103:20 reminds us, who do God's bidding and obey God's word.

This reference to "holy" angels provides the occasion to note that in this book we will be discussing exclusively "good" angels. According to Christian tradition, "the devil and his angels" are really angels who through sin fell from their exalted place and became evil angels. Yet the Bible does not give very clear evidence of this fall. Some people think that Isaiah 14:12 is referring to the fall of the devil, especially since the old King James translation put it this way: "How art thou fallen from heaven, O Lucifer, son of the morning!" This reference, however, is not to the devil but, in poetic terms, to the king of Babylon, as Isaiah 14:4 makes clear. The NIV avoids this misunderstanding when it translates verse 12: "How you have fallen from heaven, O morning star, son of the dawn!"

The best evidence the Bible gives that the devil and his hosts are fallen angels is found in Jude and 2 Peter. Jude 6 says: "And the angels who did not keep their positions of authority but abandoned their own home . . . " This verse has its parallel in 2 Peter 2:4: "For if God did not spare angels when they sinned . . . " The biblical evidence for this view of Satan as a fallen angel is not overwhelming, yet it may be adequate.

This teaching may also be supported by the fact that upon occasion the Bible does use the term "angel" to refer to the followers of Satan. For example, Revelation 12:7-9 describes a war in heaven in which Michael and his angels fight with "the dragon and his angels." Michael and his angels prevail, and so the latter are said to lose their place in heaven and to be hurled down to earth. Some scholars have understood these verses to refer to the original fall of the devil and his angels from heaven, but this interpretation cannot be correct. Rather, the passage refers in a poetic and dramatic way to the victory that Christ won on the cross over the evil powers, as the context (see especially verses 1-7 and 10-12) clearly shows. In this battle, the dragon's henchmen are referred to as "angels," thus supporting the idea that the devil or Satan and his associates are fallen angels.

Most of the time, however, when the Bible uses the term "angel" to refer to one or more extraterrestrial messengers, it is referring to "good" angels. These "good" angels, not the "evil" angels, will be the subject of this study.

Individualistic Beings

Humans, according to the Bible, are organically related to one another in that we are all descendants of "one person," as Acts 17:26 and Romans 5:12-21 indicate. Furthermore, we are intimately related to a specific family because we are born from human parents who themselves come from parents, and so on.

As far as we can tell, such organic relationships do not exist among angels. At least that is how I understand the teaching of Jesus recorded in Mark 12:25. In response to a question of the Sadducees about marriage in the resurrection, Jesus says: "When the dead rise, they will neither marry nor be given in marriage; they will be like the angels in heaven" (or see parallel passages Matt. 22:30; Luke 9:35-36). What seems to be underlying this teaching is the understanding that angels do not participate in marriage the way we humans do. There are no "little" angels who are born from other angels, no "good" angels who serve God as their parents did.

The fact is, there seem to be no "male" and "female" in the angelic world. All of the references to angels in the Bible seem to be male: "he" is the personal pronoun used, and the angels generally take on the bodily appearance of men when they are used to tell the gospel story of the coming of the kingdom. (Interestingly, today when we want a group to sing as "a choir of angels," we choose females for the parts. Either our idea of angels has changed, or males no longer are able to convey that they are a choir of angels!) The important thing to consider is that whatever commitment angels have to one another, their clear and total commitment is to the service of God and the revelation of the coming kingdom.

Announcement to the Shepherd (Angel detail)

—Lorenzo Lotti

CHAPTER 3

NAMES AND TITLES OF ANGELS

In earlier times names often revealed something important about a person. Generally, that's not true today. My first given name is Andrew. It originates from one of the Greek words for "man," or "husband." Therefore at least one dictionary suggests that it means "manly, strong, and brave." I like to think that when my parents named me Andrew, they were being prophetic—they could foresee that I would be manly, strong, and brave.

In fact, my parents named me Andrew because that was my father's name. And my father had that name because it was supposed to be the closest English equivalent to the Dutch/Frisian name that he was given as a baby ("Anne"). So much for my fantasy.

However, biblical names often (but not always) *do* give us a clue to some characteristic or function of the bearers of the name. And that's as true for angels as it is for humans. To be sure, the Bible gives us "personal" names for only two angels: Michael and Gabriel. (If one accepts the so-called apocryphal books as part of the biblical canon, then another "personal" name must be added to the list: Raphael, from the book of Tobit. And if one includes 2 Esdras under the apocryphal books, another name occurs: Uriel.) But other designations, such as the term "angel" itself and titles such as "sons of God," also tell us something about these heavenly ambassadors of God's kingdom. We'll look at many of those biblical names, titles, and designations in this chapter.

Names and Titles

Angel

Both the Hebrew word *mal'akh* and the Greek word *angelos*, from which we get the word *angel*, mean "messenger." These terms were used to refer to the messenger or the ambassador in human affairs, the one who spoke and acted as the representative of the one who sent him.

In the Bible the term "angel" also sometimes describes human messengers, but more often it is used to speak of heavenly messengers. Angels are God's messengers who speak and act as his representatives.

Perhaps here it should be noted that we received the word "angel" through the Latin translations of the Bible. The word *angelus,* not originally a Latin word, was used consistently to designate these heavenly messengers, and another more common word was used to indicate earthly messengers. Our English translations of the Bible have generally followed the same practice. For example, our English translations of Luke 7:24 have something like "the messengers of John" where the Greek uses the words "the *angeloi* of John." But in Luke 2:9, where the Greek is "an *angelos* of the Lord," our English translations have "an angel of the Lord."

In both places the word itself means "messenger." But we continue to follow the Latin practice of calling heavenly messengers "angels" and using another term, such as "messengers," for human representatives.

Sons of God

The angels' special status before the Lord is indicated by the designation "sons of God." In Job 1:6 (also in 2:1) we are told that "the sons of God" (NIV: "angels") came to present themselves to the Lord, and that Satan also came with them. In Job 38:7 all the "sons of God" (angels) shouted for joy along with the morning stars who sang. The reference to angels as "sons of God" in Psalm 29:1 is hidden behind such translations as "O mighty ones." Angels are also referred to as "sons of God" (NIV: "heavenly beings") in Psalm 89:6.

Sometimes angels may simply be referred to as "gods," as in Psalm 82:1, though this may be a reference to early rulers (see vv. 6-7). In these instances there seems to be an Old Testament pictorial idea of "the heavenly council" or "the heavenly court" in the midst of which the God of Israel reigns. See in this connection also Psalm 89; verses 5 and 7 refer to the "assembly" or "council" of "the holy ones."

Remember that in the Old Testament, Israel and the king of Israel sometimes also were referred to as the "son of God" or "sons of God." A common feature in all instances (whether of angels, or Israel, or the king) is their special status before the Lord.

Special mention must be made of Genesis 6:1-4. Here the "sons of God" married the "daughters of men" and gave birth to the "mighty ones" or the "Nephilim." The interpretation of "sons of God" here is usually understood in one of two ways:

- "Sons of God" were men who were believers in God and who married unbelieving women (thus, the "daughters of men") and who together produced offspring tending toward power and wickedness

- "Sons of God" were angels who cohabited with women ("daughters of men") and thus produced the Nephilim or the mighty ones. (In some Jewish literature this story is used in connection with the fall of the angels.)

Either interpretation has its strong and weak points. Both have something to do with the sinfulness of humanity to which the Lord God reacts. Since the interpretation of this passage is uncertain, one ought not attach much significance to its possible teaching about angels.

Spirits

In the previous chapter we tried to search out the significance of Hebrews 1:14, where angels are called "ministering spirits." We will not repeat that discussion here, but we should note that in the Old Testament the designation "spirits" was not applied to the angels. That term began to be used in the literature of the intertestamentary period and was also used occasionally in the New Testament (in addition to Heb. 1:14 and 1:7, see Acts 23:8-9 and possibly Heb. 12:9). However, the New Testament more commonly uses the term "spirits" to refer to demons, thus to Satan and his evil followers (for example, Mark 1:23; Matt. 8:16; Luke 8:36; Acts 19:13-16; 1 Tim. 4:1; Rev. 18:2).

But as we noted earlier, the passages in Hebrews 1 indicate the significance of this term as applied to angels: they are beings who have real existence and who normally do not have bodily form.

Holy Ones or Saints

We have already mentioned Psalm 89:5, 7, where angels are referred to in the expression "the assembly [or: council] of the holy ones." In Daniel 8:13 "a holy one" and "another holy one" deliver an interpretation of Daniel's vision (see also Dan. 4:13, 17, 23). Angels as "the holy ones" are also God's attendants in his coming on "that day" according to Zechariah 14:5. Most likely the term has the same sense also in Deuteronomy 33:2 (but in verse 3, "saints" refers to people).

In the New Testament, "saints" or "holy ones" almost always refers to humans who are believers. But in Jude 14, the phrase obviously refers to angels, and in 1 Thessalonians 3:13, where it speaks of the coming of Christ "with all his saints," the reference may be to angels.

Holy ones or saints are those—both angels and humans—who have been set apart for the service of God.

Watchers

The term "watcher" or "watchman" appears only in Daniel 4:13, 17, 23, and the NIV translates it as "messenger." Presumably the term means either "guardian" or "one who carefully observes" and therefore "watches." The first two references occur in the vision of Nebuchadnezzar, and the third is in Daniel's retelling of the vision. So I am not confident that the Bible intends this to be a significant description of an angel.

There is more reason to be careful about using this phrase with reference to angels: in some intertestamentary writings (the book of Jubilees and the Dead Sea Scrolls) the word "watchers" is used for evil spirits, not angels. So the term "watchers" has little relevance for understanding the Bible's teaching on the nature and function of angels.

Special Groups of Angels

Cherubim and Seraphim

The singular of these words is "cherub" and "seraph," and the plural is either "cherubs" and "seraphs" or, more often in the Bible, following the Hebrew, "cherubim" and "seraphim." (The old King James Version unnecessarily added an "s" to the plural: "cherubims" and "seraphims".)

The Bible nowhere specifically states that these are special groups of angels, but several factors make it seem likely that they are:

- The cherubim and seraphim in the Bible have angelic status and functions.

- In later Jewish literature closely allied with the Bible, the terms were used to designate beings intermediate between God and humanity.

The original meaning of these two words is too uncertain to be of help; we must rely on the biblical descriptions themselves.

The term "seraphim" is used only once in the Bible, in Isaiah 6:1-7, where we find an account of Isaiah's vision of the Lord, high and lifted up, seated on the throne, and the train of the Lord's robe filling the temple. Above the throne were the seraphim—six-winged creatures, using a set of two wings for covering their faces, two for covering their feet, and two for flying. Chanting antiphonally, they announced the holiness of the Lord: "Holy, holy, holy is the Lord Almighty; the whole earth is full of his glory." So powerful was this announcement of the *Trishagion* (the "Thrice Holy") that it shook the doorposts of the temple, filled the temple with smoke, and greatly affected the prophet, who made a confession of his uncleanness. Then one of the seraphs brought a live coal from the altar and touched Isaiah's lips, declaring his guilt to be taken away and his sin atoned for. Here the seraphim have both a prophetic function of proclaiming God's holiness and a priestly function of cleansing a prophet's uncleanness, guilt, and sin.

The term "cherubim" occurs frequently in Scripture. One can distinguish four distinct but related kinds of occurrences:

- After sin had separated the original human pair from God, cherubim were stationed east of Eden with flashing swords to guard the way to the tree of life (Gen. 3:24).

- Cherubim, apparently two-winged creatures, were associated with the dwelling places of God—the tabernacle and the later Solomonic temple—in two ways:

  —First, two cherubim were connected with the ark of the covenant in the holy of holies. In the tabernacle they seem to be placed on top of the ark overlooking the mercy seat (Ex. 25:17-22). In the Solomonic temple they were larger creatures, with wings stretching from side to side in the holy of holies, and the ark of the covenant was placed beneath them (1 Kings 6:23-28; 2 Chron. 3:10-13). This association with the ark of the covenant became descriptive of the God of Israel as the one who "dwells" or is "enthroned" "between the cherubim" (see, for example, 1 Sam. 4:4; 2 Sam. 6:2; 2 Kings 19:15; 1 Chron. 13:6; Ps. 80:1; 99:1; Isa. 37:16). The single New Testament reference to "cherubim" occurs in Hebrews 9:5, where they are described as "cherubim of the Glory, overshadowing the place of atonement."

  —Second, cherubim are mentioned in connection with the artwork in the tabernacle, specifically in the veil separating the holy place from the holy of holies (Ex. 26:31-35; 2 Chron. 3:14). Since the tabernacle was built by Moses according to the plan that God showed him on the holy mountain (Ex. 25:40; see also Heb. 8:5), it is clear that the earthly dwelling places of

God, tabernacle and temple, reflected the heavenly dwelling: God is the one who dwells between the cherubim.

- Cherubim are pictured in a highly complex vision of Ezekiel. In Ezekiel 1, we read of four living creatures, each with four faces (of a man, a lion, an ox, and an eagle), four wings, and a wheel with eyes. In Ezekiel 10 we find what appears to be a similar vision, only now the living creatures are called cherubim, and they are associated with the glory of the Lord leaving the temple (see also Ezek. 11:22). Perhaps it is from this mobile image (the cherubim and their wheels) that the Old Testament sometimes uses the picture of God riding and flying on the cherubim, as on the wings of the wind (see 2 Sam. 22:11; Ps. 18:10). In a later chapter of Ezekiel (41), cherubim are also included in the artwork gracing the promised new temple.

- In John's description of his vision of God's throne room, he doesn't use the word "cherubim." But the four living creatures that he sees surrounding God's throne are much like Ezekiel's cherubim (see especially Rev. 4:6-11). As in other places in his vision, John sees images much like those given in the Old Testament, but with peculiar differences. These living creatures do not have four faces, but each of them is like one of the faces of Ezekiel's living creature—one like a lion, one like an ox, one like an eagle, and one like a man. And instead of two wings or four wings these creatures, like the seraphim of Isaiah 6, have six wings. It is also significant that these living creatures, similar to the seraphim of Isaiah 6, sing the *Trishagion* (the "Thrice Holy") day and night: "Holy, holy, holy is the Lord Almighty, who was, and is, and is to come."

It seems quite clear that the four living creatures of Revelation combine something of Ezekiel's cherubim and Isaiah's seraphim. Obviously, cherubim (and seraphim) are an essential part of seeing the throne of God in proper perspective.

Archangels

This term, which literally means "chief angels," is used only twice in the Bible. In 1 Thessalonians 4:16 Paul says that accompanying the coming of the Lord from heaven will be three, probably related, powerful sounds: a loud command, the voice of an archangel, and the trumpet call of God. In Jude 9, Michael is described as the "archangel" who did not arrogantly presume power to himself in his dispute with the devil but said, "The Lord rebuke you!"

But though the word appears only twice, the idea of an "archangel" may occur elsewhere. For example, in Daniel 10:13, Michael is called "one of the chief princes;" Revelation 8:2 refers to "the seven angels who stand before God" and who are given the seven trumpets; and Revelation 18:1-2 describes an angel as coming down from heaven, having great authority, exhibiting a splendor that illuminated the earth, and shouting with a mighty voice.

Though "archangel" means something like "chief angel," we should be careful not to read too much into this term and assume we can carefully distinguish and classify all the orders of angels. Medieval theologians alleged that there were nine orders of intermediate spirits (listed from highest to lowest in rank): seraphim, cherubim, thrones, dominions, virtues, powers, principalities, archangels, and angels. But much of this ranking was apparently based on speculation. The Bible only mentions groupings of angels without specifying rank and numbers. And, according to Calvin and other theologians, we should be content to do the same, recognizing that such matters are part of the mysteries that will be revealed on the Last Day.

This is probably the most appropriate place to consider the two named angels, Michael and Gabriel. Michael is called an archangel in Jude 9, and if the "one who looked like a man" in Daniel 10 is really Gabriel (as seems likely—compare Dan. 10:4-6 with Dan. 9:21 and 8:15-16), then Gabriel and Michael are associated (Dan. 10:13-14). Besides, they are closely associated in the later Jewish literature of Bible times.

Just a word about their names. In Exodus 23:21, God tells Israel that he will send an angel with them on the way to the promised land, to whom they should indeed pay heed, "since my Name is in him." As if to reflect that truth, the name of "God" (*El*) is "in" each of these angel's personal names: "El" at the end of each name is the name of God in Hebrew. Thus we have Micha*el* and Gabri*el* (and in other Jewish literature, Rapha*el*, Uri*el*, Sari*el*, etc.). Michael probably means, "Who is like God?" and Gabriel means either "man of God" or "God is strong." (Raphael means "God has healed," and Uriel probably means "God is light.")

Michael appears in the book of Daniel as the one who has a special task as the champion of Israel against the rival angel of the Persians (10:13, 20). In Daniel 12:1, he leads the heavenly armies against all supernatural forces of evil in the last great battle.

This theme of Daniel 12:1 is taken up in Revelation 12:7-12, which describes the beginning of that great battle between Michael and his angels and the dragon (also identified as "the ancient serpent, the devil, or Satan") and his angels. Michael and his angels prevail against the dragon, so he and his angels are cast down to the earth and from there still continue the battle against believers. Michael's victory in heaven is symbolic of the victory of Christ on the cross (see "by the blood of the Lamb," v. 11), who effectively takes away the case of this "accuser" of Christian believers.

In Jude 9, Michael is recognized for his modesty and restraint (unlike the leaders who were tyrannizing the church to whom Jude is writing). Michael did not arrogantly take to himself the right to rebuke the devil; rather he relied on the power of God and said to the devil: "The Lord rebuke you!"

Gabriel also appears in Daniel, but primarily as a heavenly messenger (who makes his appearance like a man, Dan. 8:16; 9:21). He comes to interpret a vision that reveals the future and to give understanding and wisdom to Daniel himself (8:17; 9:22).

In the New Testament, Gabriel is mentioned only in the birth narratives recorded in Luke 1. Here too he is primarily a heavenly messenger who brings good news and thus reveals the future. He appeared to Zechariah (Luke 1:11-20) to announce the good news of John's birth. He also announced the task and function of John the Baptist, who would come "in the spirit and power of Elijah" to prepare the way of the Lord. Later Gabriel appeared to the virgin Mary (Luke 1:26-38) to announce good news. He interpreted Mary's future by explaining her role in the impending birth of Jesus and by reassuring her of her favored status before God. He interpreted Jesus' future role by declaring his status ("he will be called the Son of God") and his future rule as the son of David ("he will reign over the house of Jacob forever; his kingdom will never end").

Principalities and Powers

The apostle Paul uses the word "angel" some fourteen times in his writings. But he also refers to angels using other terms. For example, in Colossians 1:16 (NRSV) he says, "Whether thrones or dominions or principalities or powers." These are all terms used in the Jewish literature of Paul's time to refer to differing groups (sometimes for different "classes" in a hierarchy) of angels. Since Paul's presentation of these groups entails some difficult problems of interpretation, these "principalities and powers" will be discussed later in chapter 10 of this study.

The Annunciation (Angel detail) —Baldovinetti

CHAPTER 4

MESSENGERS OF GOD

If you're a member of a church with a multiple-staff ministry, you've probably drawn up or read a few job descriptions. Like most businesses, churches are growing in their awareness of the importance of having each job defined. Pastors, secretaries, ministers of music, custodians—each needs to know rather precisely his or her role, function, and assigned duties.

Knowledge of our task and calling used to be more simple, it seems. A church would call a pastor and expect him or her to do the work—and both parties had a pretty clear idea of what the work would be. After all, the pastor's role was generally defined in the liturgical form for installation and in the New Testament: it included leading worship, helping to govern the church, teaching children and the youth, and providing pastoral care.

That list of duties is not a bad job description—a very good one in fact. But in our times more seems to be needed. More and more churches find it helpful to have a specific job description for each of the persons the church hires or calls.

Perhaps something similar has happened to the study of angels. Maybe we once thought that the general role of angels could be readily summed up by saying that angels are heavenly messengers who praise God and protect God's people. That's not a bad description—a very good one in fact. But if we look more carefully, we will discover a wider diversity of parts in the biblical "job description" for angels. Each aspect is worthy of some attention.

In the next chapters of this study we will be discussing five aspects of the role that angels play. As we noted above, the Bible has a lot more to say about angels' function or role than about their "nature." But here too it will be important to study the functions of angels in the context of their calling as heavenly ambassadors of God's kingdom and rule.

Before we begin, another introductory word may be helpful. How are we to think of the myriads of angels and their various roles? I have found it helpful to think of angels organized as an army. After all, the Bible refers to them as the "hosts" of heaven, and in the Bible "host" is basically a military term. Even the familiar Luke 2:13 passage uses a military term: "a multitude of the heavenly host" is more literally translated as "a great company of the heavenly army."

An army is under orders from its commander-in-chief. A good soldier, says Paul, does not get entangled in civilian affairs but rather tries to please his commanding officer (2 Tim. 2:4). Angels are like that.

Armies are also divided into various corps, divisions, and battalions, some of which have different functions. There are infantry divisions, artillery divisions, armored divisions, and so on. There are even special service battalions who provide recreational opportunities for the fighting personnel. Perhaps when we think of angels, it may be helpful to think of them "organized" in a somewhat similar fashion. It has been helpful for me to do so.

Messengers of God

In chapter 3 we noted that both the Hebrew and Greek words that are translated "angel" really mean "messenger." Classical Greek used the word *angelos* for the messenger or ambassador in human affairs who speaks and acts in the place of the one who sent him. When the Bible applies that term to heavenly messengers, it keeps the same meaning: the ones who are God's representatives or ambassadors and who speak and act for God who sent them.

Earthly Representatives

Sometimes when we think of "messengers," we have a rather strong conviction that they are really unimportant. "Only a messenger" we often say—as if messengers were sort of office "errand boys" or "gofers" who are low on the pay scale and have little responsibility other than to bring written notes or oral requests from one person to another.

But even a quick survey of how the Hebrew word for "messenger" (*mal'akh*) is used in the Old Testament should disabuse us of this "light" understanding of the term. It clearly refers to a very responsible person, a kind of ambassador who represents in speech and action the one who sent him.

This special sense of "envoy" aptly represents the first time the term is used to designate in one passage both the heavenly messengers from God and those earthly messengers sent by Jacob to secure the favor of Esau. In Genesis 32:1-2 we are told: "Jacob also went on his way, and the angels [literally: messengers] of God met him. When Jacob saw them, he said, 'This is the camp of God!'" In the very next verse we are told: "Jacob sent [human] messengers ahead of him to his brother Esau" and instructed them very carefully as to what they should say in the hope of winning back the favor of Esau. Jacob's future security depended heavily on these messengers speaking and acting exactly according to their instructions.

Other examples underscore the responsible role of the earthly messenger:

- Messengers often represent a king; for example, Saul sent messengers to Jesse to ask that David be sent to the court (1 Sam. 16:19).

- A prophet is sometimes called the Lord's messenger—one who gives the Lord's message to the people (Hag. 1:13) or who will prepare the way before the Lord (Mal. 3:1—note that Malachi means "my messenger").

- Twice the priest is called a messenger from the Lord (Mal. 2:7; Ecc. 5:6).

- By prophetic intimation Jesus is ultimately referred to in Malachi 3:1 as both "the Lord" and as "the messenger of the covenant." (In the Greek text of Isaiah 9:5—which in this instance differs considerably from the Hebrew text from which our English translations are taken—the promised "child" and "son" is referred to as "the messenger of the great plan.")

So a human messenger (*mal'akh*) was a responsible representative of the sender—and so, too, the angels as messengers of the Lord. In the New Testament the word *angelos* refers to an earthly messenger only six times. Three times it is used in quoting Malachi 3:1 as being fulfilled in John the Baptist (Matt. 11:10; Mark 1:2; Luke 7:27). Once it is used of messengers from John the Baptist to Jesus (Luke 7:24) and once of messengers sent by Jesus to prepare his way toward Jerusalem (Luke 9:52). In James 2:25, the Greek word for "messengers" is used (NIV: "spies") for the men whom Rahab hid by faith (the Hebrew word for "messengers" also appears in the Rahab story in Joshua 6:17, 25). In the other 169 instances where it appears in the New Testament, *angelos* refers to a heavenly messenger or "angel."

Heavenly Representatives

Like human messengers, angels never speak or act simply on their own. They only and always speak for and act in behalf of God, their Sender.

Perhaps no passage in the Bible speaks as clearly as Exodus 23:20-22 of the close relationship between an angel and his Sender. God says: "See, I am sending an angel ahead of you to guard you along the way and to bring you to the place I have prepared. Pay attention to him and listen to what he says. Do not rebel against him; he will not forgive your rebellion, since my Name is in him. If you listen carefully to what he says and do all that I say, I will be an enemy to your enemies and will oppose those who oppose you."

God not only says, "my Name is in him," but also implies that by listening carefully to what the *angel* says, Israel will be doing what *God* says. Whatever originality and imagination angels may possess, they do not use those gifts to make up their own lines but only to express as effectively as they can what God wants them to say and do.

Heavenly Messengers and the History of Redemption

Angels do not appear consistently throughout the telling of the gospel story in the Old and New Testaments. But often their role as heavenly messengers is indicated at strategic points in the history of redemption.

In the Old Testament there are three such instances: in the establishment of the seed of Abraham, in Israel's exodus from Egypt and establishment in the land of Canaan, and in the return of the remnant from Babylonian exile. In the New Testament there are also three such strategic points in the life and ministry of our Lord Jesus: at his birth, at his resurrection, and at his coming again upon the clouds of heaven.

Old Testament Role

Angels as heavenly messengers play a prominent role in the establishment of the seed of Abraham.

In this story the "angel of the Lord" first appears in connection with Hagar and her descendants (Gen. 16—the question of the identity of this "angel of the Lord" will be discussed at the close of this chapter). The angel not only finds Hagar but also interrogates her, issues orders to her, and gives a promise to her. Even when Hagar and Ishmael are sent away, the angel of God appears to comfort her (Gen. 21:17).

Heavenly messengers also play an important role in other parts of this story by announcing the upcoming birth of Sarah and Abraham's son as the true "heir" of Abraham (Gen. 18:1-15), negotiating over Sodom and Gomorrah and the saving of Lot and his family (Gen. 18:16-19:29), stopping Abraham from sacrificing Isaac (Gen. 22:11-17), securing a wife for Isaac (Gen. 24:7, 40), and providing enrichment and security for Jacob and his children (Gen. 28:12; 31:11; 32:1; 48:16).

From the Old Testament we are made aware of the important role of "Abraham and his seed" in the history of redemption. The New Testament reinforces that truth (see, for example, Gal. 3:6-29). The angel of the Lord adds luster to this great event in the gospel story.

Angels as heavenly messengers also figure prominently in Israel's exodus from Egypt and establishment in Canaan.

An angel or the angel of the Lord functions as a heavenly messenger in the exodus by being involved in the calling of Moses at the burning bush (Ex. 3:2), by safeguarding Israel at the crossing of the Red Sea (Ex. 14:19; see also Num. 20:16), by being charged by God with the leading of Israel in the wilderness (Ex. 23:20-23; see also Ex. 32:34; 33:2; Judg. 2:1-4), and by confronting Balaam (Num. 22:21-35).

Strangely, the angel of the Lord is not mentioned in Deuteronomy or in Joshua. In the book of Judges the angel of the Lord acts as a heavenly messenger to establish Israel in the land of Canaan: he calls Israel to repentance at Bokim (Judg. 2:1-4); he calls Gideon to his task (Judg. 6:11-22); and he announces the birth of Samson to Mr. and Mrs. Manoah (Judg. 13:2-25).

The exodus is not only the actual redemption of Israel from the land of bondage; it is also a symbol of the more complete redemption of God's people from the bondage of sin (for example, Heb. 9:15-28). In this story the role of the angel reminds us of God's mighty intervention in the redemption of his people.

Heavenly messengers figure significantly in the return of Israel from exile in Babylon.

- An angel saved Shadrach, Meshach, and Abednego in Nebuchadnezzar's fiery furnace (Dan. 3:28) and rescued Daniel from the lions (Dan. 6:22).

- Gabriel ("one like a man") appeared to Daniel to bring messages, to interpret visions, and to give wisdom and understanding (Dan. 8:16, 17; 9:21, 22).

- The visions of Zechariah are told with an angel or the angel of the Lord appearing throughout (Zech. 1-6).

In these ways—through heavenly messengers—God was at work saving the "remnant" of his people.

New Testament Role
Appropriately, angels function as heavenly messengers in the appearance and work of Jesus, the One greater than Moses and Solomon.

Angels figure prominently at the birth of Jesus.

- Prior to Jesus' birth, the angel Gabriel announced the birth of John the Baptist to Zechariah and Elizabeth (Luke 1:11-25).

- The same Gabriel appeared to Mary to tell her she would give birth to the Son of God (Luke 1:26-38).

- An angel appeared to Joseph with instructions concerning the birth of Jesus (Matt. 1:20-24).

- An angel, with considerable help from a great company of the heavenly army, announced to the shepherds the birth of Jesus in the city of David (Luke 2:9-21).

- An angel brought messages to Joseph and Mary, urging their escape into Egypt and later their return to Israel (Matt. 2:13-20).

- The angels add power and glory to the gospel (Luke 2:10): "Do not be afraid. Behold I bring you good news of great joy that will be for all people!"

Angels announce and explain the resurrection of Jesus.

- In Mark 16:5-8 "a young man" announces the resurrection to the women who visited the tomb.

- In Matthew 28:1-7 "an angel of the Lord" rolled away the stone, put fear into the hearts of the guards, and proclaimed the news of the resurrection to the women.

- In Luke 24:1-7 "two men" "in dazzling apparel" (later identified as angels, 24:23) announce to the women the good news of
  the resurrection according to Jesus' own prediction.

The resurrection is a mighty turning point in the history of
redemption. It provides the foundation for Jesus himself saying:
"All authority in heaven and on earth has been given unto me.
Therefore go and make disciples of all nations. . . . And surely I will
be with you always, to the very end of the age" (Matt. 28:18-20).

*We know from many Scripture passages that angels will be involved in
the coming of Jesus upon the clouds of heaven.*

To what extent angels as messengers will be involved in the second coming is not clear. Paul seems to suggest in 1 Thessalonians
4:16 that it will be the "voice of the archangel," along with a great
shout and the trumpet of God, that will call the dead in Christ to
life again when the Lord himself descends from heaven. The heavenly messengers also have a role to play at the time when the one
seated on the throne says, "I am making everything new!" (Rev.
21:5). (Chapter 8 will look at angels and the second coming in
greater depth.)

In all these cases, in both Old and New Testament, angels
announce the coming kingdom of God. They do so at strategic
times and places in the history of redemption, and they do so as
the ambassadors of God, speaking and acting in his name.

Who Is the Angel of the Lord?

Who is the one usually referred to in the Bible as "the angel of
the Lord" (also called "the angel of God" or "the angel of the presence")? Members of the early church believed that this angel was
the *Logos*, a kind of temporary pre-Incarnation of the second person of the Trinity. There was some reason for that interpretation,
of course—much of it connected to the way the angel is referred
to in the Old Testament (particularly Genesis through Judges): on
the one hand the angel is distinguished from the Lord himself; on

the other hand—and sometimes in the same passages—he is identified with the Lord.

For example, in the account of confronting Hagar (Gen. 16) the angel of the Lord gives a divine promise to Hagar in the first person: "I will so increase your descendants that they will be too numerous to count" (v.10) and is identified by Hagar as "the God who sees me" (v.13). To Jacob, the angel says: "I am the God of Bethel . . . " (Gen. 31:13). Yet in securing a wife for Isaac, Abraham clearly distinguishes the angel from God: "He [the LORD] will send his angel before you" (Gen. 24:7).

Three main arguments for the view that "the angel of the Lord" refers to the divine being himself follow:

- He explicitly identifies himself with "the Lord" on various occasions.

- Those to whom he makes his presence known often recognize him as divine.

- The biblical writers themselves often call him "the Lord."

Yet many church fathers and theologians, while sympathetic to this early church view (still held by some scholars today), have argued that it doesn't really fit the evidence. In fact, St. Augustine thought this view played into the hands of the Arians (who argued that Christ was not one in essence with the Father, but a created being). He and others, such as John Calvin, believed that the "angel of the Lord" was really a created being known as an angel.

Some arguments for the view that "the angel of the Lord" refers to a created being follow:

- God often invests his ambassadors with his character and word so that they become identified with God's message.

- The prophets exhibit this kind of close relationship by identifying God's message with their own message.

- The "angel of the Lord" appears also in the New Testament and certainly as a finite creature. Yet his actions (for example, Acts

12:7, 15) are also described as an act of the Lord himself, and he sometimes speaks in the first person for the Lord himself (Rev. 22:6, 7, 12).

The arguments for and against these two positions are too technical to be considered here in detail. (For those interested in them, an excellent presentation is found in an older but thorough work by G. F. Oehler, *Theology of the Old Testament*.) My own position is that neither of the views clearly satisfies all of the data in the Old Testament. From the perspective of the New Testament it is better to say that Christ was present in the Old Testament in more than one way. The apostle Paul says, for example, that "the rock" that followed the Israelites in the desert "was Christ" (1 Cor. 10:4). So Christ did manifest himself to the Old Testament people of God, but in a variety of ways: in the rock, in the "shekinah" or cloud, but also in "the angel," who was then a finite creature through whom Christ made his presence known.

That is also Calvin's position, if I understand him correctly. Of course, a Calvinist does not always have to agree with the views of John Calvin, but it's sort of nice when it happens.

Nativity (Angel detail)

—J. Daret

CHAPTER 5

THOSE WHO PRAISE GOD

Anyone who reads the Psalms knows that angels praise the Lord. Or if they do not, they surely should. The first few verses of Psalm 148 call on all creatures—in the heavens, in the sea, and on the earth—to praise the Lord. And that includes angels:

Praise the LORD.
Praise the LORD from the heavens,
    praise him in the heights above.
Praise him, all his angels,
    praise him, all his heavenly hosts.

The reasons for this praise are given in verses 13 and 14:

    for his name alone is exalted;
    his splendor is above the earth and the heavens.
He has raised up for his people a horn [i.e., a king],
    the praise of all his saints,
    of Israel, the people close to his heart.

The angels' praise also figures prominently in the hymns of the church—and not just at Christmas, when we might expect it. For example, in the fourth stanza of the stately hymn "Immortal, Invisible, God Only Wise," the church sings: "We worship before you, great Father of light,/ while angels adore you, all veiling their sight." The hymn's writer, Walter C. Smith, obviously wants us to think that the worship and praise of the church community joins with the adoration given by the angels.

So the church is aware that the angels praise God. Indeed, "praising God" is probably one of the first things we think of when we consider the biblical "job description" of angels.

Do Angels Sing?

Many of us have never considered that question before. We've just always pictured the angels singing their praise to God. If for no other reason, our Christmas songs have told us that's the way it is. We love to sing: "Hark, the herald angels sing,/ 'Glory to the newborn King!'" Or: "Angels we have heard on high,/ singing sweetly through the night. ... "

But *does* the Bible give evidence of angels singing? Not very directly, I'm afraid.

I became aware of this fact during my first year of ministry. I decided that my Christmas Day sermon that year would focus on the multitude of the heavenly host praising God (Luke 2:13-14), and I announced the title of my sermon about a week in advance as "The First Christmas Carol."

Much to my surprise, when I began investigating the text more closely as part of my sermon preparation, I noted that the English translations were being true to the Greek text when they translated Luke 2:13 as the heavenly host "praising God and *saying*." And the Greek word for "saying" is the common ordinary word for the speaking that humans do. By itself, it has no hint of "singing" in it.

No problem, I thought—even though I was taken aback: *I can easily find other passages in the Bible that say angels "sing."* Much to my surprise, I could not find any. Remember, those were the days (1955) before the publication of the NIV and many other modern versions which occasionally translate according to the sense of the context and therefore sometimes translate the word "saying" with the word "singing." Check, for example, the NIV translation of Revelation 5:12, which says, speaking of angels, "In a loud voice they sang." The Greek, however, literally states: "*saying* with a loud voice."

The upshot of it was that on Christmas Day I used that sermon title, "The First Christmas Carol," but I had to admit to the congregation that, much to my surprise, I could find no explicit biblical warrant for the assertion that angels sing.

Today, some forty years later, I might have preached that sermon a little differently. On one level, it is still true that I can find no specific passage in the Bible that explicitly says angels "sing." But there is, it seems to me, some implicit evidence for the angels' song.

First of all, though the Greek word for "saying" by itself does not include the idea of singing, neither does it specifically exclude it. For example, in Revelation 5:9, speaking of the four living creatures and the twenty-four elders, the Greek text literally says: "And they sang a new song, *saying. . .* " From this text it is clear that "saying" does not exclude "singing." Thus, singing is not necessarily excluded from the "praising God and saying" of Luke 2:13.

Second, from the Old Testament, especially the Psalms, it is clear that "praising God" often included singing. Out of the many passages (at least twenty-nine), note just three:

- Psalm 68:32: "Sing to God, O kingdoms of the earth, sing praise to the Lord."

- Psalm 147:1: "How good it is to sing praises to our God."

- Psalm 138:1: "I will praise you, O LORD, with all my heart; before the 'gods' [probably 'angels'] I will sing your praise."

Praise of God is not limited to but does include singing. Thus Luke 2:13 might be understood, similar to Revelation 5:9, as "singing praise to God and saying."

Third, the "heavens," which may include the angels, are called upon to "sing." See, for example, Isaiah 44:23 and 49:13.

Fourth, Revelation 5:9 specifically says that the four living creatures and the twenty-four elders "sang a new song, saying." In a previous chapter, we noted that the "four living creatures" of Revelation 4 and 5 are a composite of the "cherubim" of Ezekiel 1 and 10 and the "seraphim" of Isaiah 6. It is most likely that the cherubim and seraphim are categories of angels. It is possible that the twenty-four elders—whom we will discuss further in chapter 10—are also "angels." If that is true, then we have clear evidence that at least some angels sing.

Fifth, in 1 Corinthians 13:1, Paul says, "If I speak with the tongues of men and of angels. . . " "Speaking in tongues" was a problem in the church at Corinth. Here, in the first part of verse 1, Paul is probably giving his view of speaking in tongues. If that is the case, then speaking in the "tongues of angels" probably reflects the understanding that the speaker was communicating in the dialects of heaven. From a Jewish source and from what Paul says explicitly in 1 Corinthians 14:15 ("I will sing with my spirit, but I will also sing with my mind"), it was probably understood that the tongues of angels included singing.

As nearly as I can tell, those five facts are the extent of the biblical evidence for angels singing. Clearly the evidence is implicit, partial, and inferential. But I do hope it proves the point. It's difficult for me to think of angels not singing. So I continue to understand Luke 2:13 in this way: "And suddenly there was with the angel a great company of the heavenly army, singing praise to God and saying . . . " A large segment of the "special services" division of the heavenly army were busy that night. And they had a great chorus: *Gloria in excelsis Deo.*

Angel Praise

Early Old Testament

We noted earlier that one of the first things Christians think of in the angels' job description is "praising God." And, it's true that the idea of angel praise is found in many parts of the Bible. But I was surprised to find that it is not found in the earliest books of the Old Testament—that is, from Genesis to Judges.

For one thing, this early literature most often speaks of "an angel" in the singular: the "angel of the Lord," the "angel of God," and so on. And, as we saw in an earlier chapter, that angel is usually presented as a *messenger*, one who represents God in words and actions.

When these early books do refer to angels in the plural, they are not involved in praising God. Certainly that is so in the problematic reference to the "sons of God" in Genesis 6:1-4, but also in these other instances:

- When Jacob sees the "angels" at Bethel (Gen. 28:12), they are uniting earth and heaven, but there is no mention of them praising God.

- In Genesis 32:1, the "angels" who met Jacob are seen as God's "hosts" or God's "camp," who provide protection for Jacob.

- In Deuteronomy 33:2, the ten thousand "holy ones" are God's attendant witnesses as he appears in his judicial glory.

- In Joshua 5:13-15 the "man," probably an angel, is "the commander of the Lord's army."

Psalms and Prophets

The phenomenon of angels praising God, so absent in the earlier books of the Old Testament, becomes prevalent in the writings of the prophets and especially in the Psalms.

It is in the book of Job (38:7) that we first hear of angels ("sons of God") being present at God's creation of the world. As is often noted, angels are not explicitly mentioned in the accounts of creation in Genesis 1 and 2. It is possible that they may be implicitly referred to in terms of the "heavenly council," in the plurals used in Genesis 1:26 ("Then God said, 'Let *us* make man in *our* image, in *our* likeness. . . . ' ") But since there are other possible explanations of these plurals, we cannot be certain that they are references to the heavenly council of angels. Job 38:7 tells us that at the creation the angels shouted for joy, joining the morning stars who sang together.

In the psalms we have a picture of the angels, who form the church above, standing at the head of the choir of the universe, where they adore God in the heavenly sanctuary (Ps. 148:2;

150:1). This picture of heaven as a holy temple is first found in a psalm ascribed to David (Ps. 11:4: "The LORD is in his holy temple; the LORD is on his heavenly throne"). It is also found frequently in the prophets (Micah 1:3; Hab. 2:20; Zech. 2:13; Isa. 63:15).

Especially significant is Psalm 89:5-7, which refers to the "holy ones" and to the "sons of God" who make up the heavenly "assembly of the holy ones [or: saints]." The holy ones are constantly praising and adoring God for the wonders of his grace, especially for his gracious acts in choosing the house of David. A similar picture of the angels as the adoring church above is found in Psalm 29, where they are described (v. 1) as "sons of God" [NIV "O mighty ones"] and are called upon to ascribe to the Lord glory and strength. Indeed in verse 9, because of what the "voice of the Lord" does on earth, it is said: "And in his temple all cry, 'Glory.'"

New Testament

In the New Testament only the book of Revelation presents the picture of angels as a choir in the heavenly sanctuary praising God. To be sure, Luke 2:13-14 describes the multitude of the heavenly army who praise God. But there are few references in the New Testament to this phenomenon of the heavenly choir other than in the book of Revelation. (Possible additional references are Hebrews 1:6 and Hebrews 12:22, which refer to myriads of angels "in joyful assembly.")

In the book of Revelation, as in the Psalms and the prophets, heaven is pictured as a temple. Of course, in the end of all things, in the new Jerusalem, there will be no temple (Rev. 21:22). But until that time, references are made to God's temple in heaven (Rev. 11:19; 15:5-8). Incidentally, I suspect that we Protestants do not often think of heaven as a "temple." At least, when I have suggested this biblical image of heaven to seminary classes and other groups, I have met with resistance. Perhaps it is too "priestly" for our tastes. But the picture of heaven as the "temple of God" is clearly present in the Psalms, the prophets, the book of

Revelation, and, I think, also in Hebrews (see Heb. 8:1-5; 9:11-12, 24; 13:10).

To think of heaven as a temple does not cancel out the idea that the church on earth is also God's temple (1 Cor. 3:16). On the contrary, in both the Old and New Testament the earthly temple is seen as a counterpart to the heavenly sanctuary.

Already in Revelation 4 and 5, the four living creatures (as we noted, a composite of the cherubim of Ezekiel and the seraphim of Isaiah), sing the "Thrice Holy" and do so "day and night," never stopping (Rev. 4:8). The twenty-four elders also lay their crowns before the throne and sing praise to God for his works in creation (4:10-11). Then the "Lion of the tribe of Judah" and the "Root of David," who is also the once-slain "Lamb," the one worthy to take the scroll from the right hand of the One seated on the throne, arrives in heaven. And the four living creatures and the twenty-four elders sing that new song, saying:

You are worthy to take the scroll
    and to open its seals,
because you were slain,
    and with your blood you purchased men for God
    from every tribe and language and people and nation.
You have made them to be a kingdom and priests to serve
        our God,
    and they will reign [or: "do reign"] upon the earth.

This song in Revelation 5:9-10 is extremely important for many reasons, including the fact that it gives us a glimpse of how the author of Revelation sees the interdependence of heaven and earth. Because of what the Lamb did on earth (he was slain, purchased people for God, and made them kings and priests), he was found to be worthy in heaven to take the book from the One sitting on the throne and to open the book's seals. We know from the next chapters in Revelation that the Lamb is therefore in control of things that happen in the world and to the church. The four living creatures and the twenty-four elders celebrate the activity of the Lamb. Thus from now on the praise in the heavenly sanctuary usually includes praise and worship to the Lamb, as well as to the One sitting on the Throne.

And to the grand chorus of praise from the myriad of angels in Revelation 5:11-12 and the praise of every creature in heaven and on earth recorded in Revelation 5:13, the four living creatures, standing in the Amen-corner, say "Amen." The twenty-four elders fall down and worship.

A parallel combination of praise ascending both from the human and the heavenly saints is recorded in Revelation 7. There John sees a multitude that no one can count (probably the same as the 144,000 sealed in 7:1-8, but now seen from a glorified perspective). Revelation 7:10 records the victory shout of this innumerable multitude: "Salvation belongs to our God, who sits on the throne, and to the Lamb"; Revelation 7:11-12 describes the corresponding shout of the angels, the four living creatures, and the twenty-four elders: "Amen! Praise and glory and wisdom and thanks and honor and power and strength be to our God for ever and ever! Amen!"

A similar combination of earthly and heavenly praise, but now with a grand "Hallelujah chorus," is found in Revelation 19:1-8. This is the only place in the New Testament that the word "Hallelujah" (or "Alleluia" in some versions) is found. God's work on earth is celebrated in heaven.

So Make a Joyful Noise

What we learn from all these passages is that God will be praised! We, the church on earth, are called to praise God and to blend our praise with the praise of the "saints" in the heavenly sanctuary. We should not want to miss being a part of this great choir. Even those of us whose singing is of the "joyful noise" variety certainly want to join those above who also "shout for joy."

Our God and the Lamb are worthy!

Jesus of St. Gregory (Angel detail)   —Unknown (School of Avignon)

CHAPTER 6

GUARDIANS OF BELIEVERS

Mothers with small children often believe in guardian angels. One mother I talked to lived on a busy street. Her children were absolutely not allowed to cross that street unattended by an adult. One early evening she left her three-year-old son—we'll call him "Paul"—with his father while she went for a walk. She had crossed the busy street but was still quite close to home when she heard the noise of a "big wheel" on the sidewalk behind her. It was little Paul, grinning happily. He had evidently escaped the notice of his dad and crossed the busy street.

"Paul," she asked, trying to hide the fear in her voice, "how did you get across the street?"

"It was easy," he said, smiling. "I just closed my eyes and prayed for the angels to keep me safe."

Neither Paul nor his mother doubted that the angels had done just that.

A Clear Biblical Teaching

Sometimes when I'm speaking about angels to a church group, I will quote from memory, without giving the source, a version of Psalm 91:11-12: "For he will command his angels concerning you to guard you in all your ways; they will lift you up in their hands, so that you will not strike your foot against a stone." And if I then ask, "Who said that?" the first and usually prevailing answer is: "the devil," or "Satan."

That answer is correct, of course. The devil did quote (misquote?) these words when he tempted Jesus to cast himself down from the pinnacle of the temple (Matt. 4:6; Luke 4:10-11). This episode gives rise to the oft-quoted saying: "Even the devil knows how to quote Scripture."

But it's more important to remember that the first person who said these words was the believer in Psalm 91 and that this passage has become the classic biblical support for the belief in guardian angels. These words about God's care through angels—as the little word "for" in verse 11 indicates—support the affirmations found in Psalm 91:9-10: "If you make the Most High your dwelling—even the LORD, who is my refuge—then no harm will befall you, no disaster will come near your tent."

Notice that the psalm says: "He will command his angels concerning you." Thus God uses angels to protect the believer from harm and disaster. God provides *his* care for us *through* them.

Psalm 91 does not stand alone in its teaching. Psalm 34:7 says: "The angel of the LORD encamps around those who fear him, and he delivers them." This verse speaks of the security that God provides for his people, both individually and collectively. The reference here to the "angel of the Lord" should also remind us that in the early books of the Old Testament, Genesis through Judges, there is frequent reference to an "angel of the Lord" who provided security for God's people. Think of God's promise to the people at the exodus (Ex. 23:20): "See, I am sending an angel ahead of you to guard you along the way and to bring you to the place I have prepared." Think of how the two "men/angels" saved Lot and his family out of Sodom and Gomorrah (Gen.19:1-22). Or think how the "angel of the Lord" protected Isaac at the time of God's testing of Abraham (Gen.22:9-18). Think also of how the angels of God met Jacob on his way to meet with Esau and provided the sense of security that Jacob needed when Jacob confessed: "This is the camp of God" (Gen. 32:1-2).

And we certainly cannot bypass the story found in 2 Kings 6:8-23. The king of Aram (Syria) was at war with Israel and was attempting to capture the king of Israel. Elisha the prophet was furnishing clandestine information to the king of Israel, warning him of the places where the king of Aram was setting his traps. So good was the information that the king of Aram thought he had a spy in his own ranks. When told by his advisers that it was really the prophet Elisha who was advising his enemy, the king of Aram decided to send a strong force, including his cavalry, to capture Elisha. At night they surrounded the city.

When Elisha's servant awoke in the morning and saw the Aramean army with horses and chariots, he was understandably afraid. "Oh, my lord, what shall we do?" he asked Elijah. "Don't be afraid," the prophet answered. "Those who are with us are more than those who are with them." Then Elisha prayed that his servant's eyes might be "opened"; and with opened eyes the servant looked "and saw the hills full of horses and chariots of fire all around Elisha." The Aramean forces were struck down with blindness, led into Samaria, and finally defeated by kindness from the king of Israel.

"Those who are with us are more than those who are with them" is a truth meant to give security and comfort to God's people.

The New Testament also provides many examples of guardian angels. After his temptation in the wilderness, Jesus was with the wild animals, "and angels attended [or: "ministered to"] him." Later, at Jesus' arrest, Peter, attempting to protect his master, drew his sword and cut off the ear of the high priest's servant. Jesus told him to put away his sword and said, "Do you think I cannot call on my Father, and he will at once put at my disposal more than twelve legions of angels?" (Matt. 26:53). Jesus knew that "those who are with us are more than those who are with them"; but he also knew that, according to Scripture, he was to submit to his arrest and death.

Jesus knew that God's angels were available for protection and security not only for himself but also for God's little ones: "See that you do not look down on one of these little ones. For I tell you that their angels in heaven always see the face of my Father in heaven" (Matt. 18:10). We will come back to this text a little later, but clearly Jesus means to say here that the guardian angels of "these little ones" have the undivided attention of his Father in heaven.

A Tough Question

At about this point in one of my lectures on angels, some of my listeners are bound to raise an objection. They gladly admit that the Bible clearly teaches that there are guardian angels. But that raises a problem in their minds: What about Christians who are not spared from harm or disaster? What has happened to their guardian angels? Do guardian angels take days off?

At the heart of such questions is this core question: Why are some people kept from harm and danger while others are not, and how is that related to the function of angels as guardians?

On one level that is an easy question to answer, but on another level, it is very difficult. The easy part relates to the function of guardian angels. Remember that when we looked at Psalm 91:11-12, we noted that guardian angels never act "on their own." God is the one who "commands" his angels concerning believers. Angels, including guardian angels, only do what God tells them to do. So when we question why some little child of the kingdom was not protected from harm, we ultimately are questioning the will of God.

Before we start asking "why?" about the will of God, let's face an often-heard objection to the answer that I just gave. I have contended throughout this study that angels never do anything "on their own" but only and always do God's will. Psalm 91:11-12 and other Scriptures support that notion.

But many people are not satisfied with the idea that angels never act on their own. Perhaps that's because they think along the lines of today's business model. They picture a chief executive officer (God) who gives department managers (angels) quite a lot of leeway, as long as they (department managers/angels) get the job done.

Or maybe some dislike the Scriptures' teaching because they think that such complete obedience is boring—that it makes angels into some sort of celestial robots and doesn't allow them any creative input. Perhaps they are forgetting that in the new heaven and the new earth those who are saved "will not be able to sin." We will be able only and ever to do the will of God—just like the angels.

I personally do not find that prospect boring. And I don't think angels find it boring either.

But we must return to the question: if all things happen according to God's perfect will, why are some believers saved from disaster while others are not? This is a valid question, whether God works directly or through the agency of angels. But on this side of heaven, it's a question that's very difficult to answer. We are often confronted with tragic accidents in the lives of believers and their children, and we ask the Lord over and over: Why? Why? Why?

I know of no easy answers. I do know that we as Christians have at the heart of our faith the cross of Jesus—a cross of suffering and even shame. And God did not prevent that suffering from happening to the One of whom he said: "This is my beloved Son." So the tragedy of suffering somehow fits within the confines of God's love. We must never give up on that love—even when we suffer.

Special Angels for Children?

Earlier we looked at Jesus' words in Matthew 18:10: "See that you do not look down on one of these little ones. For I tell you that their angels in heaven always see the face of my Father in heaven." This verse often raises an interesting question: "Is there a special contingent of guardian angels assigned to the care of the children of the kingdom?"

Traditionally that has been the understanding of this text. Furthermore, as I indicated at the beginning of this chapter, mothers with small children somehow feel that there must be a specially caring and efficient company of angels in charge of the safety of their children. Children need such acute care.

The traditional interpretation may be correct. But it is also possible, perhaps even more likely, that "these little ones" in verse 10 refers not so much to children as to believers who have humbled themselves like little children. That is the point Jesus makes in verses 2-4: "Unless you change and become like little children, you will never enter the kingdom of heaven" and "Whoever humbles himself like this child is the greatest in the kingdom of heaven." The emphasis is upon adults who become trusting and unpretentious—"like a little child." In verse 5 the emphasis appears to be on welcoming one who is "child*like*," and in verse 6 it seems almost certain that Jesus is referring to an adult believer who is like a little child: "If anyone causes one of these little ones who believe on me to sin . . . " So the command in verse 10 probably also refers to an adult believer who has a childlike trust in Christ.

It seems more likely then that Matthew 18:10 is referring to all believers who have childlike trust in Jesus. But, of course, that does not exclude children. Children, after all, are the model of what "childlike trust in Jesus" really is. They also are under God's providential care through angels.

Are There Individual Guardian Angels?

Another question, frequently raised, is whether a specific angel is perpetually assigned to each individual believer. When the heavenly duty roster came out, was one specific angel assigned to your personal care and security?

Some people believe that Acts 12:1-19 teaches this. You remember the story: Peter had been cast into prison by Herod. The church was meeting at the home of the mother of John Mark, praying for Peter's release. Meanwhile, an "angel of the Lord" came and miraculously extricated Peter from prison (though Peter himself thought he was seeing a vision). Outside the prison, Peter became aware that an angel had rescued him from Herod's clutches. He went to the home of John Mark's mother and knocked at the outer entrance. Rhoda, the maid, came to answer the door, and announced to the praying church that Peter was outside. The church found Rhoda's announcement hard to believe: "You're out of your mind," they said. When Rhoda kept on insisting, they said: "It must be *his* angel." Finally Peter was allowed to enter and to greet the astonished church.

Even though they were "praying earnestly" for Peter's release (v. 5), they—like so many of us today—were still "astonished" to find their prayers answered in this positive fashion. But note that they said "*his* angel." This affirmation no doubt reflects the thinking of the early church gathered there. They believed that everyone had a personal guardian angel who might occasionally show himself in bodily form and who might resemble in appearance the person under his care.

So it is possible that there is a personal guardian angel assigned to each believer. On the other hand, this passage really only proves that some early Christians believed that to be the case. Since this passage is not supported by any other Scripture passages, it does not carry much weight in proving the existence of individually assigned guardian angels.

John Calvin, you may recall, said that we should say only that which is "true, sure, and profitable" about angels. And he raised the question of whether it is really "profitable" to believe in individually assigned guardian angels. He pointed out that if I am not satisfied by the fact that the whole heavenly host is watching out for me, then it is not clear what benefit I would derive from knowing that one angel has been assigned as my personal guardian.

Calvin may be right. Yet if believing that a particular angel has been assigned for your personal and perpetual security gives you the assurance of God's personal care for you, then I see no harm in holding to it. Just remember that it is really *God*'s care through the angel that gives us security.

One final word. The biblical teaching on God's care through guardian angels is not meant to make us careless or irresponsible. Do you remember when the devil quoted Psalm 91:11-12 in the temptation of Jesus (Matt. 4:5-7; Luke 4:9-12)? He was encouraging Jesus to throw himself down from the pinnacle of the temple. Jesus responded with another text from Scripture (Deut. 6:16 NRSV): "It is also written, 'Do not put the LORD your God to the test.'"

Jesus' answer is a good one for us to keep in mind.

Annunciation

—Paul Woefel

CHAPTER 7

THOSE WHO ENCOURAGE OBEDIENCE

Did you ever call a younger sibling by the name of an older brother or sister, someone whom you knew or worked with in the past? That's a mistake teachers often make, and it sometimes causes resentment. A younger sister who has been constantly compared unfavorably to her older sister who "always got good grades" or "always did everything right" will not welcome being called by the older sister's name. She resents rather than appreciates her role model.

But role models aren't always resented. A good role model can encourage us to try harder and to be better. I have often thought: "I wish I could analyze a statement or a problem like Professor X; I wish I could retain at my disposal the relevant data about an issue like Professor Y; and I wish I could, with clarity and intensity, lay out the material before the class like Professor Z." Each, in his own way, was a role model who encouraged me to try to become a better teacher.

One of the functions ascribed to angels in the Bible, it seems to me, is to encourage believers to obey God. They do this in a variety of ways: sometimes as role models of obedience, sometimes by their very presence reminding us of what is appropriate before the Lord, and sometimes by being there to confirm that what we have done is the right thing. My hope is that we will not resent, but instead appreciate angels in this role of encouraging faithful obedience to God.

"Like an Angel of God"

A few times in the Old Testament account of David, an angel of God is recognized as the epitome of some virtue such as integrity, wisdom, or commitment to God's cause. In these instances angels are not held up as role models that the person in question is urged to be like. Rather the Bible tells us that someone thinks David *is like* an angel of God because he possesses one or more of these virtuous qualities. Implicitly the angel of God is held up as the epitome of that which is good.

We first find such a comparison in 1 Samuel 29:9, where Achish, king of Gath, affirms that David is reliable, has integrity, and is as pleasing "as an angel of God." It's apparent that this king assumes that an angel of God acts with complete integrity, and that he thinks David behaved like such an angel.

Similarly, in the story found in 2 Samuel 14:1-24, Joab puts words into the mouth of "the wise woman from Tekoa," and twice (vv. 7, 20) she affirms that King David is "like an angel of God." In this case David's wisdom is singled out in "discerning good and evil" and in knowing "everything that happens in the land." Ultimately, the purpose of this story is to enhance David's standing as the ideal ruler: comparing him to an angel of God puts a higher stamp of approval upon King David.

In 2 Samuel 19:27, Mephibosheth, Saul's grandson, affirmed that David the king was "like an angel of God." Here the implication is that David, like an angel of God, would surely do what was right. Mephibosheth had as much confidence in David doing right as he had in an angel of God.

Thus this simile "like an angel of God" is used to remind us that the ideal ruler, King David, could be trusted. In modern speech we pick up this simile as a metaphor when we say to someone who has done something especially nice and thoughtful: "You're an angel."

"On Earth as It Is in Heaven"

Much more important for our purpose in this chapter is the petition that Jesus taught his disciples to pray (Matt. 6:10): "Your will be done on earth as it is in heaven." In this third petition of the Lord's Prayer, the angels function as role models who encourage obedience—something many of us may not have been aware of as we prayed these words.

In English this prayer is called the "Lord's Prayer." In many other languages it is referred to with words equivalent to "Our Father," thus repeating the words with which it begins. The English title is correct in the sense that our Lord taught this prayer to his disciples. Notice that the Lord's Prayer was given not as a sample of how Jesus himself prayed, but as a model for his disciples: "This, then, is how *you* should pray" (Matt. 6:9).

Though the occasion for teaching the prayer is different in Luke than in Matthew, here also it is intended as a model for the disciples (see Luke 11:1-4; note that several petitions, including the third, are not included in Luke's version). Clearly, then, this is how Christians should pray. Consequently, in both Roman Catholicism and much of Protestantism, the Lord's Prayer is included in the liturgy of the church and frequently in family prayers as well.

What does this third petition mean? The Heidelberg Catechism, which is a beloved confession for many of us in the Reformed tradition, gives its explanation in two parts: "Help us and all people to reject our own wills and to obey your will without any back talk. Your will alone is good." It then goes on to explain the petition further: "Help us one and all to carry out the work we are called to, *as willingly and faithfully as the angels in heaven*" (Q&A 124).

The prayer acknowledges that the angels in heaven are our role models. We are asking that we be given the strength and courage to carry out our calling "as willingly and faithfully" as the heavenly angels. "Father," we pray, "help us to do your will on earth as faithfully and willingly as do the angels in heaven."

Some Christians are against using the Lord's Prayer as a "form" prayer. They point out that many people aren't even aware of what they are praying—especially in petitions like the third. And that's true. When I mention the meaning of this petition in my lectures, people are often amazed that they've been praying about angels. On the other hand, Jesus clearly gave the Lord's Prayer as a model for us to follow. So, even if we decide against using it as a "form prayer," we really ought to include the same types of petitions Jesus incorporated in the original—and that includes a reference to angels as role models.

Nor should we regard this role that the angels play as something incidental to the Christian faith. Since our Lord himself included it among the things we should pray for, we would do well to take it seriously. If, daily or weekly, we use the Lord's Prayer, the angels figure in a very crucial way in our Christian piety. It can be a real blessing when believers, whether in their families or in their church or both, petition the Father for help in doing his will as willingly and as faithfully as the angels in heaven.

"Because of the Angels"

First Corinthians 11:2-16, a passage that deals with the roles and dress of men and women in the worshiping church, is generating a lot of discussion these days. As one who has inherited a strong gene for male baldness, I must say that I get some special comfort from this passage. Paul says at least twice that it is good for a man to have his head "uncovered" and even that it is a disgrace for a man to pray and prophesy with his head "covered." He seems first of all to be referring to the wearing of a veil, but he also clearly refers to hair as a covering. Since I have so little hair covering my head, I figure that I am just naturally "gifted" for praying and prophesying in the most acceptable manner. Let the Absaloms beware!

More seriously, note that in giving his view of the roles of men and women in the church, Paul says, "For this reason, and because of the angels, the woman ought to have a sign of authority on her head" (1 Cor. 11:10). To give the indisputably correct interpretation of this verse is most difficult if not impossible. Two issues are especially debated: the correct interpretation of the phrase "sign of authority" and the precise denotation of the phrase "because of the angels." Without considering all of the arguments pro and con, I will give what I consider to be the most likely interpretation of these two phrases.

First of all, where the NIV translates "a sign of authority" on her head, the Greek text simply has the word "authority." The problem is that it's next to impossible to make sense out of the word "authority" in this context. The preceding argument (v. 7: "a man ought not to cover his head. . . . ") seems to require that by way of contrast the woman should be veiled, that is, wear a "sign of authority" on her head. Keeping in mind this problem, it seems to me that the flow of the argument ought to have the deciding vote in choosing the meaning of the text. Thus, by metonymy (i.e., evoking an idea by using a term that has an associated notion), Paul is saying that a woman ought to have "authority" on her head—that is, "a sign of authority" or "veil."

A second problem of interpretation is the meaning of the phrase, "because of the angels." That phrase is best interpreted, like the previous one, in the context of what Paul says elsewhere, and what in a parallel sense was affirmed in the Jewish literature of that time (the Qumran literature). In 1 Corinthians 4:9, Paul speaks of angels as part of "the whole universe" before whom Paul's apostolic ministry is on display. It seems probable, therefore, that Paul assumes angels to be present in the worshiping community as "guardians of the created order." This fits with some material from the Qumran, where it is said that people with certain physical defects should be excluded from the Qumran assembly "out of reverence for the angels."

The Christian church has never adopted the Qumran idea of prohibiting people with physical defects from participating in the worship of God. On the contrary, in recent years we have come to appreciate more and more the contributions that can be made by those with physical, mental, and other impairments.

But at its better moments the Christian church has been aware that the holy angels are present in the worship service. At the seminary at which I taught for many years (Calvin Theological Seminary in Grand Rapids, MI), there is a piece of art carved from wood that pictures a Christian community at worship with angels in attendance. "Because of the angels" in 1 Corinthians 11:10 supports this symbolism. The presence of angels is meant to encourage acceptable social and religious behavior in the church's worship of God.

"Some Have Entertained Angels Unawares"

Chapter 13 of Hebrews begins, like many letter endings, with several short exhortations. The first three verses are related. The passage moves from a command about "brothers" or believers in verse 1 to verse 2, with its command about "strangers," to verse 3, with its exhortation to remember those who are "prisoners." The word "stranger" in verse 2 probably means "one who is an outsider," or "one who does not belong to the unit in which he finds himself." That meaning also fits with the motivating clause in 13:2: "for by so doing some people have entertained angels without knowing it." Thus "strangers" should be understood as people who do not necessarily belong to the household of the faith, but who are in need of hospitality.

"Do not forget to entertain strangers" carries Christian concern beyond the boundaries of the Christian faith. Hebrews 13:1 speaks of what is appropriate within the community: "keep on loving each other as brothers"; verse 2 carries it outside the Christian community: "show hospitality to strangers"; and verse 3 carries it still further to people incarcerated: "remember those in prison."

John Calvin thought that showing hospitality was a general duty among the early Christians, applicable even outside the bonds of faith. He says in his commentary on Hebrews 13:2: "This humane duty has also ceased to be properly observed among men, because the old hospitality, celebrated in history, is unknown to us, and inns have today taken the place of private hospitality." If Calvin in his day thought that the proliferation of "inns" undermined the practice of private hospitality, imagine what he might think today of our elaborate system of hotels, motels, inns, bed-and-breakfasts, cabins, trailer parks, and the like.

Calvin seems to suggest that since many in his day were rich enough to stay in inns, there was all the more reason for the

Christian community to show hospitality to the poor, people so often in need of food and shelter. His suggestion to the people of his day certainly opens up our own opportunity to obey the exhortation: "Do not forget to entertain strangers." The homeless and the poor certainly need the compassion of Christ shown in Christian hospitality.

The writer of Hebrews motivates such compassionate hospitality by adding, "for by so doing some people have entertained angels without knowing it," a clear reference to such people as Abraham and Lot. In Genesis 18, Abraham "entertained" the "three men" by providing water to wash their feet, a tree under which to rest, and food to refresh them. These "three men" were not just "men" but "angels" or "the angel of the Lord" and two other angels. We are not certain when or whether Abraham recognized the three men as angels, but we know from the rest of the story that he did, indeed, entertain angels unawares.

In Genesis 19, Lot also entertained the two angels by providing water, food, and a place to stay. Ultimately they helped Lot and his family to escape the destruction of Sodom and Gomorrah.

The author of Hebrews may also be referring to Gideon (Judg. 6) and Mr. and Mrs. Manoah (Judg. 13), who also entertained angels. But in both of those cases the stories take a surprising shift. The food is not eaten by the angel; instead, it becomes a burnt offering to the Lord (Judg. 6:20-24; 13:16-21). It is also possible that the author of Hebrews is thinking of Tobit, who, according to the apocryphal book of Tobit, entertained the angel Raphael without knowing it.

Notice that the Hebrews passage only explicitly says that some "have entertained"—past tense—angels unawares. He does not say that if we show hospitality to strangers, we also will entertain angels unawares. But that certainly is the implication of his words.

Do we "entertain angels unawares" today? I like Calvin's answer. He says, "If anyone objects that this was an unusual occurrence [with regard to Abraham and Lot], I have a ready answer in the fact that we receive not only angels but Christ Himself when we receive the poor in His Name." Down through the ages Christians have learned that hospitality to the poor results, in one way or another, in the blessing of an intimate experience of the presence of God.

Yes, angels are given to encourage faithful obedience. The hymn writer, William W. How, put it this way:

To comfort and to bless,
    to find a balm for woe,
to tend those lost in loneliness
    is angels' work below.

Tabernacle Front with Angels

—Andrea Della Robbia

CHAPTER 8

MINISTERS OF JUSTICE (1)

In his book *But That I Can't Believe,* John A. T. Robinson gives an interesting account of what we might call the "emasculation" of angels within the church and in popular thinking. He says that already in the theology of the Middle Ages angels were treated more like an intellectual puzzle than like a serious piece of theology.

Later in the Renaissance, Robinson claims, angels became domesticated, appearing as cherubs—sweet little boys with wings, whose blissful smiles bear little resemblance to their counterparts on earth. Then, during the Romantic movement, angels were sentimentalized as sexless creatures floating through pre-Raphaelite paintings and stained-glass windows.

In the process angels have become so meaningless and lacking in zest, says Robinson, that most people have dismissed them altogether. They have became a part of the fantasy world, along with fairies and Father Christmas. Robinson suggests that a survey would doubtless reveal that more people are prepared to believe in flying saucers than in angels.

Some of Robinson's judgments may be overstatements. Certainly his last suggestion may be called into question, at least as far as Americans are concerned. In fact, a recent survey indicated that some 69 percent of Americans believe angels exist—I doubt whether faith in flying saucers would score that high!

Yet it certainly is true that in popular thinking angels have become much less virile, less powerful, and more effeminate than what the Bible suggests. As we noted earlier, today it is usually women, not men, who are chosen to represent "a choir of angels." In the Bible, angels are consistently represented as male and are always referred to with masculine pronouns. And sometimes (as in the book of Revelation) angels are presented as big and powerful.

Moreover, the Bible presents angels as stout defenders of God's cause: legions of Michael's army routing the forces of Satan and his army, agents standing behind God's "law and order." By contrast, we often think of angels as roly-poly cherubs or wimpish goody-goodies.

I mention this because it may come as a surprise to you (as it did to me when I began pursuing this biblical study of angels) that in the Bible angels are so clearly represented as ministers of justice, as agents of "law and order." That subject will occupy our attention in this chapter and the next.

"For a Little While Lower Than the Angels"

Perhaps Hebrews 2:5-9 is a good place to begin. Here the writer of Hebrews takes up again (after an interlude of "exhortation" in 2:1-4) the argument about the relationship of the Son and the angels that he began developing in 1:5-14. In chapter 1 the writer uses a number of Scripture passages to argue that the Son was exalted above the angels. Now he considers the passage from Psalm 8:4-6, which, following the Greek text of the Old Testament, could read: "You [God] made him ["man" or the "son of man"] a little lower than the angels."

How does the author of Hebrews understand Psalm 8? He gives us a clue in verse 5: "It is not to angels that he has subjected the world to come, about which we are speaking." The phrase "the world to come" is similar to the phrase used in Hebrews 1:6, where it refers to the new world order (NIV: "the world") as introduced by the ascension and coronation of the Son. The clear implication of this statement is that while the present world order has been entrusted to angelic beings, the new world order is directly under the administration of the Son, Jesus Christ.

The author of Hebrews thus understands Psalm 8:4-6 to refer ultimately to the new world order for the following reasons:

- The reference to "man" and "son of man" in Psalm 8:4, says the writer of Hebrews, finds its ultimate fulfillment in the second Adam, Jesus, the true Man.

- The meaning of the Hebrew text in Psalm 8:5 is ambiguous; it could be translated as either "a little lower than God" (NRSV) or "a little lower than the heavenly beings" (NIV). The author of Hebrews followed the Greek translation of the Old Testament that understood it to refer specifically to "angels."

- The phrase translated from the Greek as "a little" could be understood in terms of rank ("a little bit") or of time ("a little while"). The author of Hebrews understands it to refer to time so that it stresses, as verse 9 indicates, the momentary character of Jesus' humiliation: "For a little while [he] was made lower than the angels."

During his time on earth, therefore, Jesus lived in this world order under the administration of the angels. By contrast, since his exaltation, he is crowned with glory and honor, and has thus inherited a name that is superior to the angels (cf. Heb. 1:4).

Both in terms of what the author of Hebrews specifically states in 2:5 and in the way he interprets Psalm 8:5, it is clear that he holds that the present world order is under the administration of angels. The background for this position is found in Deuteronomy 32:8 and in Daniel 10:13, 20, passages we will discuss in detail in chapter 10, when we deal with the question of "national angels."

Angels as Ministers of Justice in This World Order

Here and There in the Old Testament

- In Genesis 3 we have the story of Adam and Eve falling into sin and being cast out of the Garden of Eden. Then in Genesis 3:24 we are told that God placed cherubim "east of Eden" with flaming swords flashing back and forth to guard the way to the tree of life. These angels represented God's judgment that stood between fallen humanity and God's garden. The reason for their presence is given in Genesis 3:22: lest fallen man "eat, and live forever."

- In Genesis 19 angels are involved in the destruction of Sodom and Gomorrah. Although they help save Lot and some of his family, they are also the agents of the Lord in bringing destruction to those cities. It is worth noting that in Genesis 19:12-13 the angels say they will destroy this place, but in 19:23-25 it is the Lord who does it. As ministers of justice, as in all other functions, angels never act simply "on their own."

- Did an "angel of death" "pass over" the houses of the Israelites marked with blood at the time of Israel's exodus out of Egypt? And did that same angel kill the firstborn of the Egyptians? So I was always taught in Sunday school and catechism classes, but the evidence for these facts is inferential.

  Although most of the references in Exodus 12 are to the Lord himself seeing the blood and passing over homes so marked (12:13, 27), verse 23 has led scholars to the familiar "angel of death" interpretation. The verse says that the Lord will go through the land, see the blood, and pass over that house, adding: "and he will not permit the destroyer to enter your houses and strike you down." Most interpreters believe that the "destroyer" refers to the "destroying angel" (1 Cor. 10:10, for example, where a similar Greek word is translated in the NIV as the "destroying angel," though the Greek text only says the "destroyer").

  Both in Exodus 12:23 and Hebrews 11:28, then, the literal reference is only to the "destroyer." Yet, given also the account in Genesis 19 above and the reference to "a band of destroying angels" in Psalm 78:49, it seems likely that the reference is to the "destroying angel," or the "angel of death." If so, we see this destroying angel meting out God's judgment against the Egyptian oppressors of God's people.

- The Lord's angel sent to guide God's people out of Egypt is described in Exodus 23:20-23. This angel's primary function was to lead and guard the people of Israel. But a sense of "justice" also enters into the description in verse 21: "Pay attention to him and listen to what he says. Do not rebel against him; he will not forgive your rebellion, since my Name is in him." This angel of the Lord tolerates no rebellion; he favors law and order. Obedience to the angel is obedience to God.

- The account of David taking a census of Israel and Judah is given in 2 Samuel 24 (and 1 Chron. 21). David recognized what he had done and confessed his sin to God. God sent his prophet to tell David he would be punished, but that he could choose one of three punishments: three years of famine, three months of fleeing from his enemies, or three days of plagues in the land. Trusting in God's mercy more than humanity's, David chose the third option.

  The role of the angel is described in 2 Samuel 24:15-17. We are told that the Lord sent a plague on Israel, and many died. Apparently the plague was sent "by means of an. angel," because the next verse says: "When the angel stretched out his hand to destroy Jerusalem, the LORD was grieved." The Lord said to the angel "who was afflicting the people," "Enough! Withdraw your hand." Here the angel is obviously the instrument of God's judgment against Israel.

- We have a triple account of the role of the angel of judgment against the Assyrian army in the days of King Hezekiah: 2 Kings 19:35; 2 Chronicles 32:21; and Isaiah 37:37. The sequence in the 2 Kings and Isaiah accounts is the same, with some variations in the Chronicles account: Sennacherib, the king of Assyria, threatens Jerusalem with his army; the threatened Hezekiah, king of Judah, prays to the Lord; and Isaiah, the son of Amoz, sends a message to Hezekiah containing the word of the Lord against Sennacherib. 2 Kings 19:35 says: "That night the angel of the LORD went out and put to death a hundred and eighty-five thousand men in the Assyrian camp. When the people got up the next morning—there were all the dead bodies!"

  The angel of the Lord, the minister of justice, was that night also the minister of judgment against the Assyrians. Sennacherib, we are told, withdrew from Jerusalem, went back to Nineveh, and stayed there.

- An angel or angels appear also as instruments of God's judgment in Psalm 35:5-6 and Psalm 78:49. In the latter, the old King James Version speaks of God "sending evil angels among them" as agents of his anger at the time of the exodus from Egypt. But the NIV more correctly refers to "a band of destroying angels" as ministers of God's anger, wrath, indignation, and hostility. Psalm 78:43, 51 clearly indicates that this action was against Egypt at the time of the exodus.

Here and There in the New Testament

- According to Matthew's account of Jesus' arrest, Jesus rebuked his companion for taking his sword and cutting off the ear of the high priest's servant. With that rebuke he added: "Do you think I cannot call on my Father, and he will at once put at my disposal more than twelve legions of angels?" (Matt. 26:53). But Christ, in order that the Scriptures might be fulfilled, did not call for such aid.

  Was Jesus thinking of these twelve legions as guardian angels? That might well have been part of their role. But their main function was to enforce justice by repelling the injustice of Jesus' arrest.

- According to Acts 12:23 an angel of the Lord was used as the instrument of God's judgment against Herod (Herod Agrippa I, the grandson of Herod the Great). When Herod did not give praise to God but accepted divine acclaim for himself, "an angel of the Lord struck him down, and he was eaten by worms and died."

- The references in the book of Revelation to angels as ministers of justice and judgment are legion. It is impossible to treat every one of them. And because there are different methods of interpreting the book, people disagree about whether the angels' activities belong to the future or to the present time.

Some see all of the references to angelic activity in chapters 4-19 as being part of the future and thus belonging to the special time of the "great tribulation" rather than to the activities in this present world order. But I disagree. While some of the references may be to what will happen in the future, most of them refer to events in the present era, from Christ's coronation (ch. 5) to his return (20:7-15).

If the reader allows that interpretational approach, then the angels with the seven trumpets, the three angels of Revelation 14, (one with the eternal gospel; one announcing the fall of "Babylon"; and a third announcing God's judgment upon the worshipers of the "beast"), and the seven angels with the seven bowls of the seven last plagues all belong to our present world order. In one way or another they carry out God's judgments.

Revelation 16:4-7. It is very significant for our purposes that in Revelation 16:4-7, after the third angel poured his bowl on the waters, and the waters become blood, the angel in charge of the waters glorifies the justice of God by saying: "You are just in these judgments, you who are and who were, the Holy One, because you have so judged; for they have shed the blood of your saints and prophets, and you have given them blood to drink as they deserve." Then the altar responds by saying: "Yes, Lord God Almighty, true and just are your judgments." The angels are clearly recognized as ministers of God's justice and judgments.

Revelation 12:7-12. We must spend a little extra time with the "war in heaven" passage in Revelation 12:7-12, or we might miss its judicial character. The war in heaven is fought between Michael and his angels and the dragon (the old serpent, Satan, the devil) and his angels. The great dragon and his angels were hurled down to earth, and a loud voice from heaven announced the significance of this victory.

Several items should be noted: First, the *reality* of the war is appropriately affirmed, because it is part of the warfare of God's kingdom against the kingdom of darkness.

Second, the *time* of the war is important to notice. This was not the primordial battle in which Satan was cast out of heaven (whenever that might have taken place), nor is it a battle that will take place sometime in the future. Rather this is a battle that took place at the coronation of Jesus after his crucifixion. Several things point in that direction:

— Revelation 12:5 places the attack of the dragon against the woman and her male child at the time of his coronation: "and her child was snatched up to God and to his throne."

— The victory of Christians, reflected in this battle, is said to have happened in part at least "by the blood of the Lamb" (12:11).

— This interpretation would fit with what is elsewhere clearly stated in the New Testament: namely, that Christ's ministry, and especially his death and resurrection, won a victory in the heavenly realm (e.g., Luke 10:18; Col. 2:15; 1 Pet. 3:22).

Third, the *symbolism* of the battle is an important consideration. Satan is clearly referred to as "the accuser of our brothers," the one "who accuses them before our God day and night." He was hurled down, and thus no longer has access to the throne of God (as he formerly did in Job 1 and 2 and in Zech. 3:1-6).

The battle symbolizes the truth that through his blood, Jesus has destroyed the case of the satanic accusers by fulfilling the law for us and taking its curse upon himself. The apocalyptic picture of that same victory is described by Paul in Colossians 2:13-15. Only in Revelation 12:7-12 Michael and his angels are pictured as taking up the cause of justice that was established by Jesus on the cross and celebrated in heaven at his coronation.

Administrators of Justice at the End

In Luke 12:8-9 the angels appear as a kind of judicial court of the age to come. Jesus says: "I tell you, whoever acknowledges me before men, the Son of Man will also acknowledge him before the angels of God. But he who disowns me before men will be disowned before the angels of God."

More than once the Scriptures tell us that the Son of Man/Jesus will return in glory with his angels or holy ones (Matt. 25:31; 1 Thess. 3:13). At that time he will perform judgment in the world. The angels or holy ones are thus part of his judicial train, in much the same way as the "holy ones" in Deuteronomy 33:2 constitute the judicial train of the Lord when he comes from Mount Sinai. Also significant in this regard is Jesus' statement in the parable of the wheat and the tares (Matt. 13:24-30; 36-43). The Son of Man is the one who sowed the good seed, which represents the sons and daughters of the kingdom. The tares or weeds are the sons and daughters of the evil one, sowed by the devil. The harvest takes place at the end of the age, and the harvesters are the angels. The angels will weed out of the kingdom of the Son of Man everything that causes sin and all who do evil. The weeds or tares will be cast into the fiery furnace, but the righteous will shine like the sun in the kingdom of their Father.

The angels thus appear here as instruments of law and order, both positively and negatively, at the end of the age.

Committed to Justice

A Jewish writing that dates after the time of the New Testament contains an interesting story about angels and justice.

It concerns Manasseh, a wicked king of Judah for fifty-five years whose story is told in 2 Kings 21:1-18 and in 2 Chronicles 33:1-20. The story in 2 Kings does not include an account of Manasseh's repentance and restoration, but the story in 2 Chronicles does. In Chronicles we are told that the Lord brought out the Assyrian army. The Assyrians took Manasseh prisoner and tortured him cruelly.

Through these experiences, Manasseh humbled himself and prayed earnestly to God (a prayer said to be contained in the apocryphal book, *The Prayer of Manasseh*). Moved by Manasseh's entreaty, God restored him to his kingdom in Jerusalem; we are told: "Then Manasseh knew that the Lord is God."

According to the Jewish legend, the angels resisted God in showing grace to Manasseh. They were of the opinion that such grace was not compatible with justice in this case. Such a wicked king, who only repented near the close of his life after fifty-five years of doing evil in the sight of the Lord, surely did not "deserve" forgiveness and restoration.

This legend goes beyond anything we have in the Bible itself in pitting the angels as ministers of justice over against God's forgiving grace. But it is interesting in that it picks up the theme of angels being committed to justice—a theme that we have been able to trace in both Old and New Testaments.

Last Judgement (Angel detail)

—Prevost

CHAPTER 9

MINISTERS OF JUSTICE (2)

Those of us in my generation who studied, even just a little, the English romantic poets, were probably assigned to read the poem "Abou Ben Adhem," by Leigh Hunt. (Some of us may have actually studied it!) Abou Ben Adhem, "may his tribe increase," so the poem goes, "awoke one night from a deep dream of peace" and discovered a recording angel by his bedside keeping record of the names of those who loved the Lord. Upon discreet inquiry, Abou found out that his name was not among them. Abou, somewhat taken aback, nonetheless requested a kind of "second-best" of the angel: "I pray thee then,/ Write me as one that loves his fellow-men."

When the angel returned the next night, he showed Abou, the one who loved his fellow men, the names of those whom the love of God had blessed: "And lo! Ben Adhem's name led all the rest."

In his book *The Angels and Us*, Mortimer Adler quotes a verse by B. J. Boothroyd that comments with humorous insight on Hunt's poem:

Abou Ben Adhem's name led all the rest . . .
    Prompting the thesis wildly theoretical
That even recording angels find it best
    To keep us alphabetical.

More seriously, John Ronner (*Do You Have a Guardian Angel?*) suggests that such legends of recording angels may be true at least to the extent that our own minds do the record-keeping within our memories—and even do a perfect job of it. He bases his suggestion on reports of near-death experiences and other evidence.

We saw in chapter 8 that in the Bible angels *are*, both positively and negatively, ministers of justice—and as such are very aware of the right and wrong we do. In this chapter we continue our focus on that general subject by noting that the angels, especially in New Testament teaching, are closely associated with the giving of the Mosaic law. They are said to have "spoken" or "put into effect" or "ordained" the law.

Old Testament Lawgivers

In the Old Testament angels are mentioned as part of the law-giving in only a general way. In one text they are presented as the divine judicial train that accompanied the Lord at the giving of the law. Deuteronomy 33:2 says: "The LORD came from Sinai and dawned over them from Seir; he shone forth from Mount Paran. He came with myriads of holy ones [here: angels] from the south, from his mountain slopes." Thus the angels are active in the giving of the law, according to this verse, but more in the sense of a judicial council attending the Lord who gave the law.

Similar angelic involvement in law-giving is indicated in Psalm 68:15-18, which celebrates God's ascent to Mount Zion. The psalm contains many statements that are difficult to interpret and translate. The NIV is probably correct in translating verse 17 as follows: "The chariots of God are tens of thousands and thousands of thousands; the Lord has come from Sinai into his sanctuary."

Like the author of Deuteronomy 33:2, the psalmist says that the angels accompanied the Lord God who had given his law at Sinai. Here, however, rather than serving as a judicial council attending the Lord, they are pictured as a heavenly army—the chariots of God, vast in number (see also 2 Kings 6:17).

Thus the angels are presented as adding glory, luster, and power to the presence of the Lord, the giver of the law.

New Testament Lawgivers

Given these Old Testament precedents, it is not altogether surprising that New Testament writers became more specific in their description of the role of the angels at the law-giving at Sinai.

Acts 7 contains Stephen's speech before the Sanhedrin. In his own unique way, Stephen rehearsed to the Jewish leaders a version of the history of redemption, beginning with Abraham. When he spoke of Moses, he exhibited a significant interest in the role of angels in the calling of Moses and in the giving of the law on Mount Sinai.

In Acts 7:30 Stephen affirms that "an angel appeared to Moses in the flames of a burning bush in the desert near Mount Sinai" (in Ex. 3:2, the angel is referred to as the "angel of the LORD"). Both accounts indicate that although Moses "saw" an angel, he "heard" the Lord's voice.

In Acts 7:35, Stephen interprets Moses' calling thus: "He was sent to be their ruler and deliverer by God himself, through the angel who appeared to him in the bush." God does the sending "through" [literally: "with the hand of"] an angel. This particular statement is not in the original account from Exodus; it is Stephen's interpretation of the calling.

In Acts 7:37-38, Stephen gives an even more remarkable interpretation of Moses' role as prophet and lawgiver: "This is that Moses who told the Israelites, 'God will send you a prophet like me from your own people.' He was in the assembly in the desert, with the angel who spoke to him on Mount Sinai, and with our fathers; and he received living words to pass on to us."

Though it is not absolutely certain, the "living words" referred to in this passage are probably a reference to the law that was passed on to the children of Israel. It should be noted that here the reference to "angel" is in the singular. It appears that these "living words" were spoken by the angel, received by Moses, and passed on to the children of Israel.

In Acts 7:51-53, Stephen accuses the Jewish leaders of his day of being just like their fathers: they have stiff necks and uncircumcised hearts and ears, and resist the Holy Spirit. Their fathers persecuted the prophets, and they themselves have murdered the Righteous One of whom the prophets spoke! Then he adds verse

53, to underscore the fact that they should surely have known better: "you who have received the law that was put into effect through angels [Greek: *eis diatagas angelon*] but have not obeyed it." ?

Here, unlike in 7:38, the reference to "angels" is in the plural. Scholars are not absolutely certain how to interpret the Greek phrase *eis diatagas*. In the previous paragraph we have given the NIV's translation. Others have suggested that it might be translated in a slightly different fashion: "you who received the law by direction of angels," in the sense of being transmitted "by God's directing angels."

In either translation the angels' involvement in the lawgiving is mentioned to add power to the law, to underscore the fact that it must be taken with utmost seriousness. Angels, as ministers of law-giving, are not to be taken lightly; or to put it the other way, the law, as ministered by angels, is not to be taken lightly.

Hebrews 2:2

Hebrews 2:1-4 is the first "exhortation" in the message of Hebrews. In Hebrews 1:5-14, the author uses several Old Testament texts to show that the Son of God inherited a name superior to that of the angels (see 1:4). After that he interrupts his argument about the Son and angels and inserts a word of exhortation, though it, too, is related to the angels and the Son: "We must pay more careful attention, therefore, to what we have heard, so that we do not drift away" (Heb. 2:1).

Why the "therefore" and why the "more careful" attention that is necessary? The writer of Hebrews grounds his statement (notice the word "for" with which verse 2 begins) in verses 2-3a, using what is called a "lesser to the greater" argument, in a conditional sentence that ends with a rhetorical question. The writer asks: "For if the message spoken by angels was binding, and every violation and disobedience received its just punishment, how shall we escape if we ignore such a great salvation?" The answer expected by this rhetorical question is "We cannot possibly escape." Why? Verses 3b-4 answer that question by spelling out clearly just how great our salvation is. We cannot, therefore, expect to ignore it with impunity.

Back to verse 2. Biblical interpreters agree that "the message spoken by angels" refers to the law given to Moses at Sinai. And though this message spoken by angels belongs to the "lesser" in comparison to the "greater" salvation of the New Covenant, the author says some very important and powerful things about the law:

- Note that, like the probable implication of Acts 7:38, the law was "spoken" by or through angels.

- That message, though "less" than our "greater" salvation, proved to be binding (Greek: *bebaios*). This binding character must be related to the angelic insistence on law and order.

- The evidence for this binding or reliable character of the law as ministered by angels is that "every violation and disobedience" under the Old Covenant "received its just punishment."

Thus Hebrews 2:2 assumes that the law was spoken by or through angels. The angels, or at least this division of the angels who stand behind the law, insist on law and order. Through their agency, transgressions of the law become apparent through "just punishment."

Galatians 3:19

Galatians 3:19 reads: "What, then, was the purpose of the law? It was added because of transgressions until the Seed to whom the promise referred had come. The law was put into effect through angels by a mediator."

The last part of this verse, in my opinion, has been widely misinterpreted. For one thing, it has been treated as if it were a separate sentence. It is not, even though the NIV translates it that way and may thus unwittingly have contributed to the common misunderstanding that the law is not from God, at least not directly, but only from the angels.

This (mis)interpretation arises, I believe, because the *grammatical form* of the text has not been properly observed. Verse 19 does not contain, as it were, four independent statements about the law. Not at all. Rather, in response to the opening rhetorical question, it makes one statement ("it was added because of transgressions") which is modified in two directions: the first a temporal modification ("until the Seed to whom the promise referred had come") and the second a causal participial clause ("since it was put into effect through angels by a mediator").

Thus, according to the grammar of the Greek sentence in Galatians 3:19, the author mentions that angels put the law into effect "because of transgressions"—not to show that the law comes only indirectly from God, as some misinterpreters insist.

It would be helpful, therefore, if we could determine the meaning of the phrase "because of transgressions." Some people, appealing to Romans 5:20, say it means that the law was added "to increase transgressions." Although that is a possible meaning, it probably interprets Galatians too much in the light of Romans. It is better to interpret the phrase in the light of what Paul says later in Galatians 3:21-25. From these verses it's apparent that "because of transgressions" might well mean "to expose transgressions."

When understood in this way, the function of the law in exposing sin as transgression is supported by the fact that it was "put into effect" or "ordained" by angels. And when Galatians 3:19 is read in this grammatically correct way, the function of angels in regard to the giving of the law is very similar to that described in Hebrews 2:2.

Thus Paul must have been aware of what the Old Testament said about angels as ministers of God's justice, both negatively and positively, a function of angels described in the previous chapter. He must also have been aware that angels were active in the giving of the law, a function described in the first section of this chapter.

Combining these traditions, Paul makes his statement in Galatians 3:19: angels put the law into effect so that the law exposes transgression. We know that Philo, a Jewish writer during New Testament times, suggests that God's direct agency appears only in doing good, while his judicial and punitive agency is left to subordinate powers or angels. Thus Paul reflects some of the thinking of his time, as well as the two strands of Old Testament teaching.

The Angels, Legal Charges, and the Christian

Romans 8:38, with its reference to angels as a power that might threaten to separate believers from the love of God, can best be understood in the context of our discussion of ministers of justice. A literal translation of Romans 8:38-39 would be: "For I am persuaded that neither death nor life, neither angels nor principalities, neither things present nor things to come, nor powers, neither height nor depth, nor anything else in all creation, can separate us from the love of God that is in Christ Jesus our Lord."

We may assume, I believe, that the reference to "principalities" [the NIV translates this word as "demons"] and then later to "powers" denotes the enemy evil powers. They then could be understood as the accusing powers, much the same as we find them in Colossians 2:15.

But how do "angels" fit in here among the forces that seem to threaten to separate us from God's love?

Some people have assumed that the "angels" referred to here must be evil angels. But that does not fit with Paul's normal usage: when he uses the term without further definition, he always seems to mean "good angels."

I suggest that Paul here refers to the angels who stand behind the law. This would fit with the judicial context of the passage that goes all the way back to verse 31: "If God is for us, who can be against us?" And again in verse 33: "Who will bring any charge against those whom God has chosen? It is God who justifies. Who is he that condemns?"

When we look at this context, we can understand that the law, and the angels behind it, might threaten to separate us from God's love—if the law were God's last word about us. But thanks be to God, it is not the last word. Jesus is the last word—the one who perfectly fulfilled the law and who bore its punishment against our sins. And that is why verse 39 speaks of the love of God "that is in Christ Jesus our Lord." No one, not even the holy angels standing behind God's holy law, can separate us from God's love in Jesus.

Some might object that this seems to place the angels, to some extent at least, over against or in tension with God and his love. But this is exactly the same tension that we find in Paul's gospel between "law" and "faith." On the one hand, the law is from God and is holy, righteous, and good (Rom. 7:12); on the other hand, it often appears as a kind of enemy from which the Christian has been liberated through the death and resurrection of Christ (Rom. 7:4-6).

A similar situation pertains to the angels who stand behind the law. They are good angels and represent God's law and order; but precisely because they represent the law, they may seem to threaten our relationship with God. Paul, however, knows that "the love of God that is in Christ Jesus our Lord" is God's good and last word to us. Thus we need not fear even the holy angels who stand behind the holy law.

Besides, Romans 8:38-39 does *not* imply that angels do not know about and rejoice in God's grace because of their commitment to law and order. Jesus knows of joy in heaven, joy in the presence of the angels, over one sinner who repents (Luke 15:7, 10). John sees and hears myriads of angels praising the Lamb who was slain and who was thus worthy to take control in heaven and on earth (Rev. 5:11-12). Here, once again, it may be helpful to think of angels as an army (the "heavenly hosts"), with some divisions particularly devoted to law and order and others especially attuned to praising the great acts of God's grace in Jesus Christ.

There is a Jewish story about David in which David says to God: "Lord of the World, to an angel wilt thou hand me over, who shows no favor [cf. Ex. 23:21]? Who can stand before him? 'If thou, O Lord, shouldst keep note of iniquities, O Lord, who could stand?' If Thou sayst that forgiveness is not in Thy power, it *is* in Thy power, as it is said, 'For with Thee is forgiveness that Thou mayst be revered' [Ps. 130:3f.]."

The Jewish writers of this story knew that angels were more on the side of strict justice than on the side of mercy. They also knew that God had it in his power to forgive. They were right; yet how much more clearly God's power to forgive is shown in the love of Christ Jesus our Lord.

The Coronation of the Virgin —David Aronson

CHAPTER 10

SOME DISPUTED ISSUES ABOUT ANGELS

Perhaps this chapter title takes you by surprise. *Some disputed issues,* you may be thinking. *I thought* most *of the issues we've considered had some points of dispute in them. I'm surprised there are any 'disputed issues' left.* I must say that I sympathize with that sentiment. In fact, for a while I even toyed with the idea of calling this chapter, "Some *Really Big* Disputed Issues."

On the other hand, I do not wish to be an alarmist. After all, remember that John Calvin reminded us that in our discussions of angels we should say only that which is "true, certain, and beneficial." I have tried to be obedient to that injunction, even though I've had to note, from time to time, that certain Scripture passages contain debatable points of interpretation.

In any event, I hope that I have now sufficiently alerted you to the fact that the passages or themes we are taking up in this chapter are in dispute—in part because data is scarce and in part because the interpretation of the available data is uncertain. In each instance I will acquaint you with the major positions of interpretation and tell you which one I prefer and why.

Are There National Angels?

Does the Bible teach that the administration of the various nations has been parcelled out among a corresponding number of angels?

According to the Greek translation of Deuteronomy 32:8, the verse should read (slightly different from our English translations based on the majority Hebrew text): "When the Most High gave to the nations their inheritance, when he separated the children of men, he set the bounds of the peoples according to the number of the angels of God." In our English translations, following the majority Hebrew text, the last line reads: "according to the number of the sons of Israel."

In this case the Greek may have the better text since it is now supported by a Hebrew manuscript fragment of Isaiah from Qumran. And what this Greek text seems to imply is that the nations have been parcelled out to a corresponding number of angels. These angels are presumably accountable for both the fortunes and misdeeds of those nations.

That implication seems to become explicit in the book of Daniel, where we meet what most interpreters consider the angelic "prince of Persia" and the "prince of Greece" (Dan. 10:13, 20). Michael is introduced as "the great prince" who champions the cause of the people of Israel (Dan. 10:13, 21; 12:1). This interpretation seems to fit with the implication of Hebrews 2:5-9—while the "world to come" is not under the administration of angels, the present world order is.

But not all scholars are convinced that angels are in charge of the world's nations. Some argue that the Hebrew text of Deuteronomy 32:8 does not refer the nations to angels, and that the "prince" of Persia (and Greece) in Daniel 10:13, 20 might not be a reference to an angel at all but to the human king or ruler (as the reference to "the king of Persia" in 10:13 might suggest).

So the issue can be argued both ways. But in my opinion, the rather clear implication of Hebrews 2:5-9 tips the scales in favor of the view of national angels. I also think this view may be behind the problematic text of 1 Corinthians 6:3. You remember that the context there speaks of the Corinthians going before civil judges with matters that they should judge themselves. Paul, in upbraiding them, affirms: "Do you not know that we will judge angels?" (In 6:2 Paul asked, "Do you not know that the saints will judge the world?") Some interpreters feel that Paul is referring to the judgment of fallen angels, as in 2 Peter 2:4 and Jude 6. But, as we noted earlier, usually when Paul uses the term "angels" by itself he is referring to good, not fallen angels.

So it seems more likely to me that Paul is here deriding the fact that the Corinthians are going before civil judges who may thus represent their national angel. Paul is saying that the eschatological people of God will judge those very angels. The church is one body in which "nationality" has been sublimated to our oneness in Christ. For, as Paul says elsewhere, in the church "there is no Greek or Jew, circumcised or uncircumcised, barbarian, Scythian, slave or free, but Christ is all, and is in all" (Col. 3:11).

This world, with its separate nations (and angels in charge of them), will have no place in the world to come, and thus the saints will "judge" those national angels.

Well, Then, Are There Church Angels?

Does Revelation 1:20 teach that each church has an angelic representative in heaven who might be said to function as its "administrator"?

A loud voice that sounded like a trumpet commissioned John to write to the seven churches (Rev. 1:11). When he turned to discover the source of that voice, he saw among seven golden lamp stands "one like a son of man." Among other things this risen, glorious, powerful One held in his right hand seven stars (1:16).

In 1:20 this Living One interpreted the vision for John saying, among other things, "The seven stars are the angels of the seven churches." In addition, the letters to the churches in Revelation 2 and 3 are addressed to the angel of that church: "To the angel of the church of Ephesus, write," and so on to each of the seven churches.

Most interpreters who believe that the Old Testament teaches that there are national angels who administer the affairs of each nation, also believe that the angels here are heavenly counterparts of the churches on earth. John, they maintain, adapted the familiar notion of national angels to the church situation. Since the other fifty-nine references to angels in Revelation (outside of these eight references in Revelation 1-3 under consideration) are to superhuman heavenly beings, they argue, we can assume that these references also point to heavenly messengers.

"Not so," say many other interpreters. The term "angel" means, as we noted earlier in chapter 4, "messenger." And it is used in the New Testament some seven times to refer to human messengers. Therefore, these scholars argue, *angelos* here refers either to the seven "human messengers" who carried the letters to the seven churches, or to the bishop or pastor of each of the churches.

The second option seems the more likely of the two since, if it were a reference to the seven messengers, it is difficult to see why the letters were addressed to the messengers rather than to the churches. As we noted in chapter 3, the Hebrew word for "angel" was used occasionally to refer to a prophet, and thus the bishop or pastor could have been thought of as a prophet. However, this would be the only place in the New Testament where the term *angelos* is used to refer to a Christian leader.

The issue is difficult, since no matter which interpretation one chooses, some problems of unique usage remain. Yet, in my opinion, the arguments supporting the reference to heavenly angels are stronger. I am not sure what "benefit" such a teaching might have, to raise Calvin's question again. Perhaps the presence of such "church" angels underscores the truth that there is in Revelation a very close tie between heaven and earth: what happens on earth has a profound effect in heaven, and what happens in heaven has a profound effect upon earth.

Are the Twenty-Four Elders a Special Class of Angels?

The twenty-four elders, though referred to elsewhere in the book of Revelation, are described in detail in Revelation 4 and 5. They are said to be seated on twenty-four thrones surrounding *the throne* and are closely associated with the four living creatures. John describes them as beings dressed in white and wearing crowns of gold on their heads.

Whom do these twenty-four elders represent? Many scholars believe they represent the church: either the ideal church in heaven anticipating the final state or the raptured church. The strongest argument in favor of this position is that in Revelation 21 the number twenty-four comes back in a sense when the new Jerusalem is described as having twelve gates (the twelve tribes) and twelve foundations (the twelve apostles) and, of course, the new Jerusalem is closely identified with the bride, the church. In addition, the word "elder" is not normally used to describe angels.

The arguments in favor of the twenty-four elders representing a special class of angels, which in my judgment is the more likely interpretation, are too technical to be given in full, but here are some of them:

- The twenty-four elders are in close proximity to the four living creatures, joining them in praise and singing the new song of Revelation 5:8-10. The four living creatures, as we saw earlier, represent a combination of Ezekiel's cherubim and Isaiah's seraphim and therefore represent a special class of angels.

- The twenty-four elders expedite the prayers of the saints ("bowls of incense," 5:8), a task which elsewhere (8:3) is ascribed to an angel.

- According to the best reading of Revelation 5:9-10, the twenty-four elders are distinguished from the church in the song that they sing, as they are also in 7:13-17 and in 14:3. Since John "sees" them seated on thrones, these twenty-four elders probably represent the "heavenly assembly" or "heavenly council" of the angels (or "sons of God") that we met in the Old Testament and briefly described in chapter 3.

What about the "Principalities and Powers" in Paul's Writings?

The phrase "principalities and powers," taken from the King James and Revised Standard versions, is the common one used to designate the "personal angelic powers" that appear in the writings of Paul (and once in 1 Peter 3:22). Paul uses five different words to name these personal powers, four of which appear in

Colossians 1:16: "thrones" (*thronoi*), "dominions" (*kyriotetes*), "principalities" (*archai*), and "powers" or "authorities" (*exousiai*). A fifth term, (*dynameis* [also often translated "powers"]) appears in Romans 8:38 and elsewhere. Thus the phrase "principalities and powers" is used for the sake of simplicity to designate the "personal angelic powers" denoted by these five terms. These beings are referred to in the following passages in Paul: Romans 8:38; 1 Corinthians 15:24; Ephesians 1:21; 3:10; 6:12; Colossians 1:16; 2:10; 2:14-15; and 1 Peter 3:22.

Several questions arise about the meaning and significance of these terms.

Where did Paul (and Peter) get these names from?

Paul seems to borrow these terms from Jewish sources that had their origins between the Old and New Testaments. These sources, in which angelology is extensively developed beyond the Old Testament writings, use the five words described above to designate angelic beings, intermediaries between God and humanity.

In medieval Christian theology the terms are used to designate five of the nine orders of angels. But the New Testament seems to use these terms interchangeably, always in connection with the work of Christ.

Do the terms represented by "principalities and powers" truly refer to "personal" beings?

One important interpreter, H. Berkhof, has argued that Paul did not think of angels as "personal" beings; after all, in Romans 8:38 he seems to place them in the same category with such non-personal entities as "present and future" and "height and depth."

But since these terms did refer to personal beings in the Jewish writings from which Paul seems to have taken them, there is no reason to doubt that Paul also used them in this sense. Or perhaps Paul considered them to be personal beings that need to be "reinterpreted" for our time. For an excellent treatment of this idea, see the three volumes of an important modern writer, Walter Wink (listed in the bibliography).

Are the principalities and powers good (angelic) powers or evil (demonic) powers?

On the one hand, these powers were created by God and created through and unto Christ (Rom. 8:38; Col. 1:16). Thus they are part of God's good creation. On the other hand, they represent part of the demonic opposition to the community of believers (Eph. 6:12: "Our warfare is not against flesh and blood but against principalities and powers. . . . "). Furthermore, they have been "reconciled," "exposed," and "subjected" to Christ (Col. 1:20; 2:15; 1 Pet. 3:22). Thus they seem to be less than "angelic."

Perhaps the best way to interpret this two-sidedness of the powers is to see that they represent the tension of the creation order: on the one side the carnal aspect of the fallen creation, and on the other the created structure as it comes from God through Christ. Even though they are fallen, the powers can represent both the positive and negative sides of the creation, for God can use even the fallenness of creation for a positive end.

Certainly the positive contributions of the powers in the creation order, (e.g., their maintenance of law and order through fallen institutions) must not be overlooked. On the other hand, when these powers assume a role beyond that intended by God, they become a threat to the well-being of the church.

This depiction of the powers as both good and evil has been challenged by one recent writer, Wesley Carr. He argues that in Paul, just as in his Jewish sources, the principalities and powers are only good angels who give homage and worship to Christ. He claims that Colossians 2:14-15 speaks not so much about Christ's victory over the powers as about Christ's lordship and its recognition by these angelic hosts. He recognizes that Ephesians 6:12 cannot be made to fit into this scheme of "good angels," so he thinks it is a second-century A.D. addition to the text. In my opinion neither Romans 8:38 nor Colossians 2:14-15 (and Eph. 6:12) can really be made to fit into his hypotheses.

What is the church's role as described in Ephesians 3:10?

This may be a good way to end our discussion of this complex problem. In Ephesians 3:10 Paul says that the church is called to make known to "the principalities and powers in the heavenly realms" the "manifold wisdom of God." The text does not say exactly how the church must fill this assignment; the context suggests that it may happen through the church's deeds (as the reconciled community of Jews and Greeks) and through its words (the proclamation in all creation of this "mystery" of Christ).

As the context shows, God takes up the church into his plan for the ages. The more the church portrays that she is the multicultural, multiracial, multinational body of Christ (as the seer John says so often, "out of every tribe and language and people and nation"), the more she makes known to the principalities and powers so closely tied to God's creation that God is indeed bringing back the unity of his original creation. The more the church proclaims the mystery of Christ and God's plan for reuniting all things under the lordship of Jesus Christ, the more she proclaims to the principalities and powers that God's gospel is still at work to "bring all things in heaven and on earth together under one head, even Christ" (Eph. 1:10).

What a glorious, exciting, challenging calling God has given to us, the church!

Meditation   —Yugo Simberg (1873-1917)

CHAPTER 11

DO ANGELS REALLY EXIST?

As I type this chapter, last week's issue of *Time* magazine (December 27, 1993) is lying before me. Its cover story is titled the "New Age of Angels." "Sixty-nine percent of Americans believe they exist," the lead-in copy states. "What in heaven is going on?"

If your first reaction was like mine, you probably thought, *Wow! Sixty-nine percent! That's a lot of people—more Christians believe in angels than I imagined!*

But after I read the article and thought about it some more, a couple of modifications began to sink in.

First of all, I realized that I had misread the statement by equating "Americans" with "Christians." As the article itself points out, a belief in the existence of angels is affirmed not only by Christians but also by Jews and Muslims (and Buddhists, Hindus, and so on). The appearance of the article near Christmas, a time when Christians speak and sing about angels more than almost any other time of year, may have led me to assume incorrectly that the article was speaking about Christian belief in angels.

A second modification settled into my evaluation. The fact that 69 percent of Americans believe in the existence of angels does not mean that 69 percent of those Americans would say that angels play a significant role in their religious faith life. Many Christians who believe that angels exist (to deny that angels exist would take away from the "magic of Christmas") have specifically told me that they rarely think about angels.

In these last two chapters we will be considering the significance of our belief in angels—not simply *whether* they exist but if and how they play a role in our conscious Christian faith.

In this chapter we will take a look at some of those who deny or almost deny the existence of angels. As we think about their points of view, please be alert to one fact: some Christians who deny the "existence" of angels still have a lively sense of the role angels play. For example, one contemporary Old Testament scholar, Claus Westermann, openly states that "there are no angels," and thus angels "have no existence," yet he wrote a very helpful and intriguing book called *God's Angels Need No Wings* on the role angels played in the Bible (and continue to play today) as the messengers of God. So be ready to find "belief" in angels even among some Christians who deny their "existence."

Near Denial of the Existence of Angels

Karl Barth affirms that angelology must articulate what the witness of Scripture offers or else it will deteriorate into "an angelology of the weary shrug of the shoulders." Then he gives an insightful overview of the positions of many nineteenth- and twentieth-century theologians that give evidence of this "weary shrug of the shoulders."

No Angels

Part of Barth's point is that only a few theologians have absolutely denied the existence of angels. These thinkers appealed to the modern view of the world, which affirms that all things come from within the world and not from the outside. They argued that this view of the cause and origin of all things makes the existence of angels not only unlikely but impossible (Barth has in mind here such persons as D. F. Strauss). It is clear that such theologians had no room for "heaven" or the "supernatural" that penetrates our world of cause and effect. Thus they dispensed with heaven and angels altogether. One of them quite cynically said: "Heaven may be left to angels and sparrows."

No Angels—Maybe

Only a few theologians made this completely negative affirmation, says Barth. But many other theologians shared this "modern view of the world" (here he thinks of F. D. E. Schleiermacher and his followers). Accordingly they believed that the supernatural world, if it exists at all, exists only in the sensual world. And they held that since we find the cause and effect of things completely within our world system, there is no room left for angels in God's ruling of the world through his divine providence. Angels, these theologians claimed, are present in the Jewish Scriptures of the Old Testament and from there simply pass over into the New Testament without becoming a specifically Christian teaching. Thus there is no need for angels, and there is no need really to discuss them theologically.

However, unlike the few theologians we looked at first, this second, larger group stopped short of completely denying the existence of angels. Although they found angels irrelevant for Christian theology, most of them tried to find a place for angels as objects of pious opinion, as elements in the symbolic speech of religions, or as symbolic representations.

I have spent this much time with this "near denial" of the existence of angels because it is not simply an interesting historical study. It represents, I believe, the position of many Christians today. For many Christians, modern science has eliminated the need for angels, maybe even made impossible the significant involvement of angels in their lives. For these people, angels have become superfluous. Such people would probably stop short of denying the existence of angels, but at the same time they consider angels irrelevant for Christian faith.

But does that make sense? It seems to me that this near denial of the existence of angels also entails the denial of the providence of God. And that seems like a high price to pay.

Happily, many Christians recognize the appropriate place of "cause and effect" within the world while at the same time affirming the truth of God's providential care. For them, belief in angels and their functions is only a step away. A stalwart Dutch theologian, Abraham Kuyper, has suggested somewhere an either/or: either we honor the world of angels as God has revealed that world in Scripture, or run the danger of falling back into a naturalistic religion, holding only to those things that we can see.

I think Kuyper is right. What do you think?

What about the claim that angelology is not a specific Christian teaching? As noted above, these near-deniers of angels sometimes hold that angels are in the Jewish Scriptures of the Old Testament and from there pass over into the New Testament without becoming a specifically Christian teaching. More recently this argument has been carried a step further: Scholars claim that angels do not need to be taken seriously as a Christian teaching because they only appear in a certain type or genre of New Testament literature, particularly the "apocalyptic" genre (for example, Revelation).

How do we respond to these arguments?

First of all, we must acknowledge that angels do appear with great frequency in the apocalyptic genre. The Greek word *angelos* occurs about 175 times in the New Testament. Over a third of those occurrences (67) are in the book of Revelation. The word also occurs twice in the so-called "little apocalypse" of Mark 13 (and twice in the parallel chapter in Matthew 24).

On the other hand, angels also appear in all the other genres of the New Testament: gospel, narrative (Acts), and epistle. In the gospels, angels appear in both the gospel writers' own material (for example, Luke 2:9-13) and in the material attributed to Jesus (for example, Mark 12:25; Matt. 18:10; Luke 12:8-9; John 1:51). In Acts, the angels appear both in the speeches of characters (for example, Stephen, Acts 7:30-38) and in the commentary by the narrator (for example, 12:7-15). The apostle Paul accords angels not only a role in the Old Testament (for example, Gal.3:19) but also in his own perspective on his work as an apostle (for example, 1 Cor. 4:9). The author of Hebrews, of course, deals with angels extensively in chapters 1 and 2, even though the main purpose of this proclamation is to show that angels are subordinate not only to God but also to the God/Man, Jesus Christ.

The reference to Hebrews 1 and 2 brings up one other important consideration. Perhaps angels do not play a more prominent role in the New Testament because they do not belong on center stage. Center stage belongs to the coming of God's kingdom in Jesus Christ. Angels are ancillary to that—they play their part "in the wings," so to speak. Angels are reticent creatures; they never draw attention to themselves but only to the God whom they serve. Even the archangel Michael, in a story recorded by Jude in verse 9, did not rebuke the devil in his own name but said rather: "The Lord rebuke you!"

It seems to me that the amount of material in the New Testament and its spread throughout the various genres is in keeping with the role angels are assigned to play.

Angels and Mythology

R. Bultmann and his followers have tried a different approach from that of the older liberal theologians, though they share the starting point of the "modern view of the world." Bultmann says that the cosmology of the New Testament is essentially mythical in character. The three-storied universe was structured with earth in the center, heaven above, and the underworld beneath. Heaven was the abode of God and of celestial beings—the angels. The earth is more than the scene of the natural, everyday events; it is also the scene of the supernatural activity of God and his angels, on the one hand, and of Satan and his demons on the other. In this mythical view, the supernatural forces intervene in the course of nature and in all that people think, will, and do.

This mythological view of the world, says Bultmann, has become obsolete for modern thinkers. It cannot be made to fit with the "modern view of the world," which holds that everything that happens has a cause in this world, and that events are not open to intervention from above or without. Bultmann is clear: "It is impossible to use electric light and the wireless and to avail ourselves of modern medical and surgical discoveries, and at the same time to believe in the New Testament world of spirits and miracles. We may think we can manage it in our own lives, but to expect others to do so is to make the Christian faith unintelligible and unacceptable to the modern world."

Bultmann's approach is not to deny the existence of angels. Nor does he simply eliminate them from New Testament teaching while keeping other aspects of the mythological world view of the New Testament. Rather, he wants to "demythologize" this worldview, to seek to understand what meaning it may have for the correct understanding of humanity. Thus for Bultmann all "theology" is "anthropology."

Although Bultmann himself does not do much to "demythologize" the angelic world in his theology, one of his followers, John A. T. Robinson, does so in detail. Anyone who has read Robinson's book *Honest to God* knows that Robinson attaches himself to Bultmann's statement of the mythological character of the New Testament world (as well as to the viewpoints of Bonhoeffer and Tillich). Robinson argues that the supernatural aspect of Christmas—God sending his Son with the angels taking part—can survive if we understand it for what it is: a myth. For Robinson myth has its legitimate place because it indicates the significance of historical events—what he calls "the divine depth of the history."

In a later book, *But That I Can't Believe*, Robinson spells out more fully his view of angels as mythology. He acknowledges once again that angels are unintelligible to modern thinkers, and in that sense they should be removed from the gospel we preach. But, he says, they still have a role as myth. What is their significance? He mentions three things:

- They remind us that there is meaning to the whole process of nature and history.

- They remind us of those forces that lie beyond the threshold of conscious control, such as the forces of the collective unconscious.

- They remind us of God's constant presence in ordinary life.

There may be some readers of this book who feel the same way about angels: they do not exist—it is impossible to believe in them and their actions as presented in the Bible—but they may help us understand the "spiritual meaning" of natural and historical events.

Personally, I find this approach both contradictory and unsatisfactory. It seems to me that either God can or cannot intervene in history. If God cannot intervene, then angels can have little meaning, no matter how hard we try to give them meaning as myth. If God *can* intervene, there is no reason why he cannot use angels as they are presented in the Bible.

Angels Do Not "Exist" Except as Messengers of God

In the introduction to this chapter, I referred to the work of Claus Westermann (*God's Angels Need No Wings*). I wanted to alert the reader to the fact that some Christian scholars deny that angels "exist" but nonetheless affirm their role as messengers of God. Westermann may speak for others who are raising the question of "belief" in angels. It seems proper, therefore, to devote some space to his approach, especially since one can learn many things from his book that Calvin might call, "true, certain, and profitable."

If those who conducted the poll described in *Time* magazine had asked Westermann, "Do you believe that angels exist?" he probably would have answered, "Of course not." Westermann explicitly says: "There are no angels. Even in the Bible there is nothing of the kind." He thinks that we should not raise the question of the existence of angels, for it is a "red herring."

Westermann also tries to avoid the question of whether God exists. He believes that one cannot get at the reality of either God or angels by raising the question of their existence. For, if I understand him correctly, he feels that when we do, we try to fit God and/or angels into our human concept of being. Angels, he affirms, have "no being in a sense comparable to what we mean when we speak of human existence."

However, Westermann does hold that there are "messengers of God," and he describes angels as such messengers. In fact, angels only "exist" in that particular role, according to Westermann. He says: "An angel is 'born' for a certain task, and when that certain task is discharged, the angel ceases to exist as such. The whole sum and substance of an angel is to be a messenger who brings a message."

Well, that's pretty "deep stuff." And you should read Westermann's book yourself before you judge whether his is a helpful way for you to think of angels.

For me it is not helpful. I believe that everything we say about God is in some way measured according to our human concept of it. That is even true of what Westermann believes in—namely, "receiving a message from God." For me, if it is appropriate to speak of "receiving a message from God," then it is also appropriate to ask whether the God from whom the message comes really "exists." Therefore I think it also appropriate to speak of God "existing" and of angels "existing," even though I recognize that in some sense I will do so in terms of my limited human conception of being. Because for me, perhaps strangely, only those things that really "exist" can truly "act."

Besides, I disagree with Westermann when he says that "the Bible never speaks of the being or existence of angels per se." In chapter 2, when we looked at what the Bible says about the characteristics or "being" of angels, I agreed with Calvin that the only way the argument of Hebrew 1 and 2 makes sense is if angels are recognized as spirits of real substance or existence. It seems to me that we are allowed to speak of their existence to the extent that the Bible does.

In the meantime, I do hope that all who read Westermann's book will have his wish fulfilled: namely, that his book "will even help the reader to hear what the Bible has to say about angels with a sense of expectation."

Angel from the Blessed Sacrament Chapel —Gianlorenzo Bernini

CHAPTER 12

THE BENEFIT OF BELIEVING IN ANGELS

As we have noted at other times in this book, John Calvin maintained that when speaking of angels, theologians should say only those things that are "true," "sure," and "beneficial" or "profitable." He meant, of course, that even though people often prefer to speculate about angels, theologians should limit themselves to what is "true" and "sure" as set forth in the Bible. Much of the discussion about angels in this "new age" seems to be speculation.

But Calvin also meant that there is no point in discussing angels unless it somehow benefits our faith. The reformer was convinced that Scripture was given to edify Christians—to shape them into persons of sound godliness, of solid trust, of proper fear of God's name, and of genuine holiness.

It is specifically the "benefit" of believing in angels that we will seek to investigate in this chapter.

What Angels Do Today

In our investigation of the "benefit" of believing in angels, we need to ask a prior question: Do angels still have all the same functions they had in biblical times?

The short answer to that question is this: "Almost but not quite." There is, however, a longer answer that may be helpful in explaining the shorter one.

You will recall that in the second section of this study, we identified five functions that the Bible ascribes to angels:

- They are messengers of God.

- They praise God.

- They are guardians of believers.

- They encourage Christian obedience.

• They are ministers of justice.

It seems to me that all of those functions, except the first, are pretty much the same today as in Bible times. The reason the first function has changed is because the role of messenger in those days was so closely related to announcing or explaining events in the history of redemption. We noted, for example, that in the Old Testament, angels played a prominent role as messengers at three critical points: the establishment of the seed of Abraham; Israel's exodus from Egypt and establishment in Canaan; and the return of Israel from exile in Babylon. In the New Testament, angels likewise functioned as messengers at three moments in the life and ministry of Jesus: at Jesus' birth, his resurrection, and his coming in judgment.

In all these events, except the final one, the angels' function as messengers had ended by the time the Bible was established as the canon for the Christian church. So, while angels may function as messengers today in a more general sense—in guarding, encouraging, confirming, and so on—they are no longer needed to announce or explain events in the history of redemption. The Bible and the indwelling Spirit now fulfill that role.

Angels Are for Our Benefit, Not God's

Why does God sometimes use angels to reveal his power, to provide for the safety of believers, and to communicate his blessings to them?

As John Calvin noted, it would be a mistake to assume that God uses angels because he needs them—as if he were somehow too weak or too ineffective to do these things on his own. Oftentimes, Calvin points out, God carries out his will and work directly, without using angels. So it is clear that *God* does not need them.

That brings us back to the original question—why angels? Calvin says, in short, that God uses angels *in order to comfort us in our weakness.* It perhaps should be enough to know that God promises to protect us. But we sometimes see ourselves surrounded by so many perils, so many enemies, so many harmful things, that we might yield to despair if God did not reassure us of divine care and protection by means of the multitude of angels.

Calvin notes that it would be wrong for us to cast doubt on the simple promise of the Lord's protection and care. If *we* did so, it would be as if we thought God wasn't really powerful enough to protect us and needed outside help. But it is quite another thing when God in his grace and kindness caters to our weakness by revealing his use of the myriad of angels on our behalf.

The distinction that Calvin makes in the preceding paragraph is very important. Otherwise we might think that we are, or should be, people of such mature faith that we are doing God a favor by not affirming the importance of his use of angels on our behalf. In fact, if we do not affirm the importance of God's use of angels we are actually refusing to accept God's provision for us in our weakness.

Let me use an example. We Christians often say that the Bible, God's Word, (or "the preaching of the Word") is the "chief" means of grace that God uses to call sinners to himself and to give them life. So it is. But then what about the sacraments, such as baptism and the Lord's Supper? They are then in some sense "secondary" means of grace. Noting this, we might conclude that we do not need the sacraments. We might even sound very pious about it: "All I need is the Word; I don't need those secondary helps." But then clearly we would be making ourselves wiser than God, who instituted the sacraments as means of grace precisely because *he knows that we need them.*

So, too, with angels. God knows that we might feel very small and fearful because of the power of our enemies. But we should never doubt God's personal care for us. Calvin shows how that has worked in the past by appealing to the story of Elisha's servant in 2 Kings 6. The Aramean (Syrian) king sent many horses and chariots to surround the city in which Elisha was staying. When Elisha's servant saw these forces, he was, understandably, filled with fear. In anguish he asked Elisha what they could possibly do against such an overwhelming foe. Then Elisha prayed, and his servant's eyes were opened; the servant saw the surrounding mountains filled with horses and chariots of fire. Then he knew the truth of the prophet's words: "Those who are with us are more than those who are with them."

So the Lord ministers to our weakness. Perhaps a modern example would be helpful. I remember, on one of my visits to Chicago, feeling very much alone and threatened. People were jostling me on the sidewalk—so many of them going in both directions and headed for so many different destinations. There were people whizzing by in cars too, and I could hear the rumble of the trains overhead, carrying another crowd of persons to a whole variety of places. Not far from where I stood was a busy airport filled with people taking off and landing.

As I stood there in that crowded place, I found myself wondering, Can God really take personal care of me and at the same time take care of all the believers on the sidewalk and in the cars and on the trains and in the airplanes? What about my wife and children in Michigan, my parents and siblings in Iowa, and my aunt in California?

Then I thought of God's angels. His myriad of angels, ten thousand times ten thousand and thousands of thousands more. Somehow "I will never leave you nor forsake you" was easier to accept and understand when I thought of God's angels all around me—and in Michigan, Iowa, Canada, and every other place on earth. "For he will command his angels concerning you to guard you in all your ways." Thank you, Lord.

Important for Our Thinking about God

This last story brings up the question of how we think about God's involvement and providential care in the world in general and in the lives of believers in particular.

In catechism classes when I was young, and later in doctrine classes in college and in seminary, I was taught to distinguish between "deism," "pantheism," and "theism." (Of course, we had not heard of "panentheism" then.) Deism and pantheism, we were told, are bad (i.e., inadequate; atheism is really bad), but theism is good (i.e., taught in the Bible and in the Reformed confessions).

Pantheism is inadequate because it does not recognize the distinction between God and the world but tends to equate them. It thereby eliminates providence in the proper sense of the word. Deism is inadequate because it tends to deny that God has a universal, special, and perpetual involvement in the affairs of the world. According to deism, God only exercises a kind of general oversight, since creation and history continue to function according to their built-in powers. The example used to teach the meaning of the deist position was that of a watchmaker. The watchmaker makes the watch, winds it up, and then lets it run in accordance with its built-in powers. In the deist position, God is the Divine Watchmaker. He created the universe with powers and laws inherently in place, then "wound it up," and has since allowed it pretty much to operate on its own. Neither position is acceptable, we were taught.

Instead, we were encouraged to be theists. Theism, we were told, is good because it distinguishes between God as Creator and the world as created. At the same time, it affirms that God continues to be involved in creation and history in three ways:

- God preserves all of his creatures.

- God directs and governs all things to their appointed end.

- God is operative in all things that come to pass in the world.

Now I think that my teachers were right; theism is good because it is taught in the Bible. It is echoed and explicated in the Reformed confessions (and in other Christian confessions as well). I confess that I am a theist. But I find that I often think and act like a deist. I know and confess that God is involved in the affairs of the world by preserving all creatures, governing history, and cooperating in all that comes to pass. But unfortunately I often think of God as exercising only general oversight. I too often tend to think of the world and history as a process that God has set in motion, and not as a vessel that God pilots day by day. Do you ever have the same problem?

In my better moments I think that the Bible's teaching on God's use of angels helps me to have a more solid view of God's involvement in the world and in my life. I find that one of the "benefits" of the Bible's teaching on angels is that it helps me think more "theistically" about God.

Abraham Kuyper made a helpful suggestion in this regard. Unfortunately, he started with a premise that I do not accept. He simply affirmed that in our day, unlike in Bible times, there are no appearances of angels to Christians. I think that is wrong; many Christians have "angel stories" to tell, stories that rest upon genuine appearances of angels. I think such experiences are real, even though not all Christians have them. But after that initial dubious premise, what Kuyper has to say gets a lot better.

His argument runs like this: Even though there are no personal experiences of angels in our times (the premise with which I do not agree), the Bible's teaching about angels is nonetheless significant for our thinking about God and the affairs of God. People might argue that if there are no personal experiences of angels, they cannot possibly be important for our faith. But Kuyper says that would be a false conclusion.

He uses an example: We do not have the personal experience of the martyrs and heroes of our history. Yet what they have done is very important for our thinking and understanding of the present. To use some examples (different ones perhaps than what Kuyper had in mind), neither you nor I, I suspect, have ever met or had personal experience of Polycarp, martyr of the early church. But Polycarp's martyrdom is important for my thinking about the Christian faith and what it means to be a good witness for Jesus Christ. Neither you nor I, I suspect, have ever had a personal experience of Abraham Lincoln. Yet what Lincoln did for our country and what he said in his Gettysburg address is very important for my understanding of the union of the American states and for my conviction that the blessings of our constitution were meant for black people as well as white.

In a similar way, Kuyper argues, even without a personal experience of angels, the Bible's teaching about angels is significant for our thinking about God. I would say that they help us to think more "theistically" about God.

Another Dutch theologian, G. C. Berkouwer, suggests something similar. In his book *The Providence of God*, he notes that Abraham Kuyper affirmed that the denial of angels came by way of denying demons and Satan. Berkouwer thinks, conversely, that with the renewed interest in the demonic in our day (for example, the question of the demonic and the totalitarian state), there may also come a better appreciation for what the Scriptures say about angels. Berkouwer knows that in the Scriptures the coming of Christ's kingdom occupies center stage. Angels are always and only "in the wings." But he thinks that a better appreciation for the scriptural teaching on angels might help us think less abstractly about God's governing of the world.

Berkouwer's opinion seems right to me. Again, I would say that angels help us to think about God in a more "theistic" way. And that is a great benefit indeed.

The Storytelling Family of God

In "The Storytelling Family of God," poet Stanley Wiersma suggests that the church, God's family, has her own story since she has been acquiring her identity throughout history. He knows that all solid families acquire their identities by the stories they tell. He ends his perceptive article with a question: "Would doctrinal controversy be so vicious and ecumenical conversation so difficult if we had thought of the church through the centuries as the storytelling family of God?" Wiersma obviously hopes that we, the church, will more and more become the storytelling family of God.

In recent times the "story" or "narrative" nature of the Bible has been emphasized. And philosopher/theologian Stephen

Crites has reminded us that angels perform an important function in the formation of that story or narrative. In fact, he maintains, angels are essentially narrative figures. That does not mean that they are, therefore, merely fictional fancies. Not at all. They appear, rather, at dramatic turning points in the Christian story.

That has continued to be true here and there in the history of church and synagogue, says Crites. He points to the astonishing musical appropriation of Bible stories among Black slaves in America and notes that "when stories sing, angels appear." On the other hand, when the narrative imagination is supplanted by religious tradition, then angelology loses its vitality. Angels tend to fade from the horizon when the religious consciousness turns away from its narrative sources.

A vital angelology may thus lead to a better telling of our story—that is, of God's way and will in our lives. Angels are essentially narrative figures, and a good story is a great benefit.

Angels as part of our story about God and God's care can help us see that "those who are with us are more than those who are with them." The psalmist in Psalm 34 could best tell the story of his deliverance from fear by telling of the campsite next to his own:

I sought God, he answered me;
   he delivered me from fear.
Look to him, your face will shine,
   free from shame and from despair.
     Lo, the angel of our God
     camps near those who fear the Lord.

—Versification by Marie J. Post

BIBLIOGRAPHY

Adler, Mortimer J. *The Angels and Us*. New York: Macmillan, 1982.

Bandstra, Andrew J. "Face to Face with Angels." *The Banner* (December 2, 1991): 6-7; (December 9, 1991): 18-19.

————— "A Job Description for Angels." *Christianity Today* (April 5, 1993): 21.

————— *The Law and the Elements of the World*. Kampen: J. H. Kok, 1964.

————— "Principalities and Powers." *The International Standard Bible Encyclopedia*. Vol. 3. Revised, edited by G. W. Bromiley. Grand Rapids, MI: Eerdmans, 1986. pp. 971-973.

Barth, Karl. *Church Dogmatics*. Vol. 3, Part 3, edited and translated by G. W. Bromiley and T. F. Torrance. Edinburgh: T. & T. Clark, 1961.

Berkhof, Hendrikus. *Christ and the Powers*. Scottdale, PA: Herald, 1962.

Berkhof, Louis, *Systematic Theology*. Grand Rapids: Eerdmans, 1949.

Berkouwer, G. C. *The Providence of God*. Translated by L. B. Smedes. Grand Rapids, MI: Eerdmans, 1952.

Bietenhard, Hans. "Angel, Messenger, Gabriel, Michael." *Dictionary of New Testament Theology*. Vol. 1, edited by C. Brown. Grand Rapids, MI: Zondervan, 1979. pp. 101-105.

Bultmann, Rudolf. "New Testament and Mythology" *Kerygma and Myth*. Edited by H. W. Bartsch. New York: Harper, 1961. pp. 1-44.

Calvin, John. *Institutes of the Christian Religion*. 2 volumes, edited by J. T. McNeill, translated by F. L. Battles. Philadelphia: Westminster, 1960.

————— *The Epistle of Paul the Apostle to the Hebrews*. Translated by Wm. B. Johnston. Grand Rapids, MI: Eerdmans, 1963.

Carr, Wesley. *Angels and Principalities.* New York: Cambridge University Press, 1981.

Crites, Stephen. "Angels We Have Heard." *Religion as Story.* Edited by J. B. Wiggins. New York: University Press of America, 1986. pp. 23-63.

Daniélou, Jean. *The Angels and Their Mission: According to the Fathers of the Church.* Westminster, MD: Newman, 1976.

Davidson, Gustav. *A Dictionary of Angels.* New York: Free Press, 1967.

Gibbs, Nancy. "Angels Among Us." *Time* (December 27, 1993): 56-65.

Gilmore, G. Don. *Angels, Angels, Everywhere.* New York: Pilgrim, 1981.

Graham, Billy. *Angels: God's Secret Agents.* Revised. Waco: Word, 1986.

Jones, Timothy. "Rumors of Angels?" *Christianity Today* (April 5, 1993):18-22.

Joppie, A. S. *The Ministry of Angels.* Grand Rapids, MI: Baker, 1953.

Kakes, H. *Waar Zijn de Engelen Nu?* Kampen: J. H. Kok, [no date].

Kittel, Gerhard. "angelos." *Theological Dictionary of the New Testament.* Vol. 1. German edited by G. Kittel. English edited and translated by G. W. Bromiley. Grand Rapids, MI: Eerdmans, 1964. pp. 74-87.

Kuyper, Abraham. *De Engelen Gods.* Second edition. Kampen: J. H. Kok, 1923.

Langton, Edward. *The Angel Teaching of the New Testament.* London: James Clarke, [no date].

——————— *The Ministries of the Angelic Powers According to the Old Testament and Later Jewish Literature.* London: James Clark, 1936.

Lockyer, Herbert. *The Mystery and Ministry of Angels.* Grand Rapids, MI: Eerdmans, 1958.

MacDonald, Hope. *When Angels Appear.* Grand Rapids, MI: Zondervan, 1982.

MacGregor, Geddes. *Angels: Ministers of Grace.* New York: Paragon House, 1988.

Oehler, Gustav. *Theology of the Old Testament.* Translated by G. E. Day. Grand Rapids, MI: Zondervan, 1983.

Régamey, Pie-Raymond. *What Is an Angel?* Translated by Dom Mark Pontifex. New York: Hawthorn, 1960.

Robinson, John A. T. *But That I Can't Believe!* New York: The New American Library, 1967.

——————— *Honest to God.* Philadelphia: Westminster, 1963.

Ronner, John E. *Do You Have a Guardian Angel?* Indialantic, FL: Mamre, 1985.

Van der Hart, Rob. *The Theology of Angels and Devils.* Notre Dame, IN: Fides, 1972.

Westermann, Claus. *God's Angels Need No Wings.* Translated by D. L. Scheidt. Philadelphia: Fortress, 1979.

Wiersma, Stanley. "The Storytelling Family of God." *Adjoining Fields: For Stanley Wiersma, A Gathering of Works and Tributes.* Edited by the Calvin College English Department. Grand Rapids, MI: Calvin College, 1987. pp. 42-46.

Wilson, J. M. "Angel." *The International Standard Bible Encyclopedia.* Vol. 1. Revised, edited by G. W. Bromiley. Grand Rapids, MI: Eerdmans, 1979. pp. 124-127.

Wink, Walter. *Naming the Powers: the Language of Power in the New Testament.* Philadelphia: Fortress, 1984.

——————— *Unmasking the Powers: the Invisible Forces That Determine Human Existence.* Philadelphia: Fortress, 1986.

——————— *Engaging the Powers: Discernment and Resistance in a World of Domination.* Minneapolis: Fortress, 1992.